IT'S ALL ABOUT MONEY AND POLITICS:

WINNING
THE HEALTHCARE
WAR

YOUR GUIDE TO HEALTHCARE REFORM

JOHN D SANDERSON

IT'S ALL ABOUT MONEY AND POLITICS:
WINNING THE HEALTHCARE WAR
YOUR GUIDE TO HEALTHCARE REFORM

iUniverse books may be ordered through booksellers or by contacting:

iUniverse
1663 Liberty Drive
Bloomington, IN 47403
www.iuniverse.com
1-800-Authors (1-800-288-4677)

ISBN: 978-1-5320-8438-6 (sc)
ISBN: 978-1-5320-8439-3 (e)

Library of Congress Control Number: 2019915023

Print information available on the last page.

iUniverse rev. date: 09/27/2019

DEDICATION

This book is dedicated to my children: Michael Sanderson, Susan Adams, Amy Babcock, and Christy Sanderson; and to my grandchildren: John P. Sanderson; Drake Babcock; Shelby Babcock; Kenny Weisenberger; Joe Weisenberger; Nick Babcock; Bria Sanderson, Chloe Sanderson and my great grandson Keith Sanderson, all of whom will pay the price if we are unwilling to fix the healthcare cost and access problems; and to my wife, Betty, without whose love, encouragement, and support I would have placed the future of my children and grandchildren in the hands of others without having voiced my opinion or tried to make a difference.

CONTENTS

PROLOGUE

In 2008 I published the book, "It's All About Money: Winning the Healthcare War!" It is time to revisit those writings. Some of the original text is included with a few minor changes. In that book I focused a lot on price versus charge issues and what I considered warring factions - hospitals, insurance companies, networks, physicians and government. I also included a section entitled "It isn't that complicated!" Although the principles outlined in that section are as true today as they were in 2008, I oversimplified them, ignored very important issues that must be taken into account, and did not provide a comprehensive and integrated proposal to implement a consumer driven system that can serve all of America's people. I also presumed that businesses and individuals had such invested interests that they would just pick up the ball and run with it. I now understand that thinking was at best naïve. It is clear to me today that any attempt to expand coverage and reduce the rapid increase in healthcare expenditures must have a buy-in from all parties – businesses, individuals, insurers, providers (hospitals, physicians, pharmaceutical companies, other healthcare service organizations) and local, state, and federal governments. Since each provider group has its own special interests and our elected officials seem to be more interested in the next election than on what is best for the people, this all-encompassing buy in falls somewhere between Herculean and impossible. However, as the crew of the NSEA Protector says in the movie *Galaxy Quest*, "Never give up! Never surrender!"

INTRODUCTION

For most of my 76 years, I owned a dog. My last dog was Phoebe, a cute little Pug with a curly tail that was wagging most of the time except when she slept. Every dog I've had wagged its tail a lot. And that is my point. The dog wags its tail. The tail does not wag the dog. I've tried to make the tail wag the dog but it never happens. Phoebe's tail could be wagging a mile-a-minute and if I grabbed it, it just stopped. I've never held a dog's tail and seen the dog start wagging. But that is exactly what is happening in healthcare today, the tail is wagging the dog. Networks direct individuals to hospitals and other healthcare service providers that charge inflated prices, so they can get big discounts that yield artificial savings and inflate administrative costs! The individual (the dog) is being controlled (wagged) by the insurance companies, networks, hospitals, governments and other healthcare service providers (the tail).

The first health insurance policies were written in London and the United States in 1850 and by 1866 more than 60 insurance companies were writing policies. The early policies covered lost income from diseases like scarlet fever, smallpox and diabetes. Healthcare insurance, as we know it today, came about in 1929 when a group of school teachers contracted with Baylor Hospital in Dallas, Texas to provide room, board, and some other services for a specific monthly fee[1].

The United States started down the path of employer-paid healthcare plans during World War II when employers used healthcare benefits as a means to attract skilled labor. A price/wage freeze was in effect and businesses were successful in obtaining a ruling that healthcare benefits could be provided as a non-wage, tax-exempt employee benefit. Following the war, labor began including healthcare benefits in contract negotiations and, because healthcare insurance was inexpensive and welcomed by all, the businesses acceded to the demands. Within a few years, healthcare benefits became part of the compensation package of most large businesses and industries and these benefits began creeping into the smaller businesses.

Although healthcare costs raised a little faster than the general rate of inflation, costs remained fairly reasonable through the early to middle 1960s. In essence, the dog (the individual) was wagging the tail (healthcare providers: physicians, hospitals, insurance, etc.). If a person needed healthcare services, he went to the physician(s) of his choice; together they decided what would be done and, if necessary, which hospital to go to; and when the bills came, the patient paid them. If insurance was involved, the patient would file the claims and receive the insurance payment. Admittedly, there were a sufficient number of individuals who were insured but didn't pay their bills after receiving their insurance benefits that hospitals and other providers started insisting on the assignment of insurance benefits.

Things changed dramatically, however, when Medicare and Medicaid were enacted as part of President Lyndon Johnson's Great Society in 1965[2]. Since the implementation of Medicare, we have

---

[1] "Health Insurance, The History:" Washington Insurance Council, 1999.
[2] Iglehart, John K.: "The American Health Care System – Medicare," The New England Journal of Medicine, January 28, 1999, Volume 340, Number 4.

gradually evolved to the tail wagging the dog. Employers choose healthcare insurance plans for the employees; the insurance plan and employers choose networks; the networks choose the physicians, hospitals, etc. along with which services and prescription drugs will be covered by the plan. Insurance companies generally claim that they don't deny their insureds access to any service, physician, hospital, pharmaceutical, etc.—they just won't pay much or anything toward it. The reality for most of us is that if the insurance plan won't help pay for it, we don't have access to it.

It is time for the power of the consumer to correct the insanely inefficient, complex, cumbersome, and impersonal healthcare business in the United States! Our other choices are more of the tail wagging the dog or a single-payer, national health plan. My perception is that most people are tired of the tail wagging the dog.

Today, slightly less than 50 percent of Americans support the single-payer, national health plan approach. My experience with Medicare and Medicaid along with my studies of national health plans in other countries, have led me to believe that all alternatives must be exhausted before going the single-payer route. Do you really want the same government that runs Medicare, Medicaid, the Veterans Administration, and oversaw the Healthcare.gov launch running your healthcare? How much freedom of choice are you willing to relinquish? How much control over you and your family do you want to give to the federal government? How much healthcare is a right versus a privilege?

Reforming healthcare in the United States is not rocket science, brain or heart surgery, but it is extremely complex and has become, in essence, a WAR! It is not a war as defined by armed conflict between nations or factions within a nation, but it is war as defined by active hostility, conflict, contention, and strife. We currently have active hostility, conflict, contention and strife within our healthcare delivery and finance programs, special interest groups, and political interests. Therefore, by one definition, we, the ultimate consumers of healthcare services, are at war with those that participate in programs that create inequities, higher costs, conflict, and strife for us.

You don't need to know how an internal combustion engine works to drive a car. You do, however, need to know a few basics to drive it safely and to keep it running. Although you don't need to know how an engine works to drive the car, the more you do know about how your car works, the less likely you are to get ripped-off when your car breaks down and needs repairs.

Similarly, you don't need to be a physician, hospital, insurance executive, or a politician to drive healthcare reform or fight the war! You do, however, need to know a few basics. And, like avoiding getting ripped-off on car repairs, the more you know about your health and the way healthcare works, the less likely you are to get ripped-off when you need professional healthcare services.

That is what this book is all about. It is to give you the basic information you need to fight and win the healthcare war. Consider it your basic training to prepare you to protect your individual rights and to fight the war for change in your business, your community, and in the political arena.

For decades most of us have been waiting for someone else to fix things. Volumes have been written analyzing nearly every aspect of healthcare in great detail. Hospitals, insurance companies, physicians, and governments have been pointing fingers at each other saying, "We are doing the best we can—it's your fault!" Think-tanks have been analyzing and proposing public policy for decades. And do you know what? Things have changed a lot, but few of the changes have helped the average person.

As noted above, volumes have been written on each specific healthcare issue but finding something that puts the whole healthcare mess together in one place is difficult. That is what I am attempting to do here - give an objective overview of the major issues involved as our country tries to improve healthcare delivery. Objectivity is key. To make informed decisions, we must be exposed to all points of view – the good and bad of each option. Unfortunately, objectivity is nearly nonexistent in mainstream news media and objective journalists are few and far between. We all have some biases and it is hard not to let them leak through in our communications. However, when expressing a biased opinion the recipient of that bias needs to know it is biased. Nothing wrong with being biased – just admit it!

You won't encounter a lot of healthcare industry jargon in this text; you won't read detailed think-tank analyses, and you won't find a long list of references. You will be given statistics and data you need to have a big picture view of healthcare in America today. You will read in simple straightforward terms my view of the issues, how we arrived at where we are today, and the actions that average working people can, and must, take to regain control of their healthcare and that of their families.

I believe the only way to win the healthcare war is to engage each person in the fight. However, before you join the fight you should view healthcare from the big picture perspective, decide not to place blame for any specific problem, and not complain about a problem without at the same time proposing a possible solution.

Hospitals and insurance companies have had decades to fix the problems and have failed. Healthcare reform has been included in political platforms since the early 1900s and our legislators have not reached consensus on solutions. If the problems in healthcare are to be fixed, it is up to us. No one else is going to do it. I and my family have to fight for what we believe is right. We have to fight the war with our physicians, hospitals, insurance companies, employers, and especially our elected officials. You and your family have to understand all of the issues and fight for what you believe is right too. You have to fight the war with your physicians, hospitals, insurance companies, employers, and your elected officials. As a country, we can solve this complex problem but it will require open discussion of the issues, the options and facts – both pro and con. I hope and pray that you will join in an informed discussion and then fight for what you believe to best solution! We are fighting to get back what is ours – our liberty and the freedom to choose!

CHAPTER ONE

WHERE WE ARE TODAY

Under current law, national health spending is projected to grow at an average rate of 5.5 percent per year for 2018-27 and to reach nearly $6.0 trillion by 2027. Health spending is projected to grow 0.8 percentage point faster than the Gross Domestic Product (GDP) per year between 2018 and 2027 bringing the health share of the GDP from 17.9 percent to 19.4 percent by 2027.[3] In 2016, the per capita healthcare expenditures in the United States were $9,892 compared to $4,192 in the United Kingdom and $4,753 in Canada.[4] Despite the US spending substantially more than other developed countries on healthcare, approximately 27.4 million (about 10 percent of the nonelderly population) remain uninsured.[5]

---

[3] National Health Expenditure Projections 2018-2027: cms.gov

[4] Organization for Economic Co-operation and Development (OECD) data: Health resources-Health spending

[5] Kaiser Family Foundation: Key Facts about the Uninsured Population, December 7, 2018

Continuing our current programs without change commits us to more of what we've experienced during the last 30-40 years. In 2017, U.S. health care costs were $3.5 trillion. That makes health care one of the country's largest industries. It equals 17.9 percent of gross domestic product. In comparison, health care cost $27.2 billion in 1960, just 5 percent of GDP. That translates to an annual health care cost of $10,739 per person in 2017 versus just $146 per person in 1960. Health care costs have risen faster than the average annual income. Health care consumed 4 percent of income in 1960 compared to 6 percent in 2013.[6] Although the Affordable Care Act signed into law in 2010 (Obama Care) did help to slow the rate of growth in national health spending to 4.8 percent from 2010 to 2017 it is still growing too fast and still approximately 27.4 million (about 10 percent of the nonelderly population) remain uninsured.[7] In 2013 one out of five American adults (56 million people) struggled to pay health care related costs. Of those, 10 million had health insurance to cover most of the costs but they couldn't meet the deductibles that average between $5,000 and $10,000 per year.

Of those who had trouble paying their medical bills, 73 percent skimped on groceries, clothing or rent. Sixty percent used up their savings. More than 40 percent took on extra work to pay the bills. Almost one in four cut back on taking their prescription medications. About 30 percent postponed getting follow-up care. That leads to further health problems down the road. Rising health care costs forced 34 percent to rack up high-interest credit card debt. Fifteen percent took out other loans, while 13 percent borrowed from a payday lender.

These families were not the poor, who are usually well-covered by Medicaid. Instead, two-thirds were homeowners and three-fifths

---

[6] Amadeo, Kimberly: The Rising Cost of Health Care by Year and Its Causes, the balance, March 12, 2019
[7] Kaiser Family Foundation: Key Facts about the Uninsured Population, December 7, 2018

were college graduates. They were middle-class Americans who got hit with massive, and unexpected, out-of-pocket medical expenses.[8]

We are spending a lot of money on healthcare with our current programs and the question, "What are we getting for our money?" must be addressed. Healthcare is extremely complex and specialized, so most of us do not know what to expect when we need healthcare or whether we were treated appropriately or optimally. Objective metrics (indicators, measures) about healthcare performance can assist individuals with their own healthcare decisions, provide context for state and national policy discussions about healthcare programs and investments, and point to where and how the system can be improved. There are more than 250 quality measures and we'll look more at quality in chapter six but at this point let's just take a quick glance at where we are today.

Comparing the overall ranking of healthcare among 11 industrialized countries (Australia, Canada, France, Germany, Netherlands, New Zealand, Norway, Sweden, United Kingdom, and the United States) the United States ranks as follows:

- Quality Care – 5
- Effective Care – 3
- Safe Care – 7
- Coordinated Care – 6
- Patient-Centered Care – 4
- Access – 9
- Cost-Related Problem – 11
- Timeliness of Care – 5
- Efficiency – 11
- Equity – 11
- Healthy Lives – 11
- OVERALL RANKING – 11

---

[8] Amadeo, Kimberly: Health Care Costs Facts, the balance, March 21, 2019

Although the United States has made good progress in some areas including five-year relative survival rate for cervical cancer, mortality rate for cervical cancer, and 30 day in-hospital mortality rate for hemorrhagic stroke, other countries outperform the United States in many areas.[9] These include:

- Overall mortality rate for breast and colorectal cancers
- Mortality rate for diseases of the circulatory system, respiratory, endocrine, nutritional, and metabolic diseases
- Premature death (Potential Years of Life Lost)
- Life expectancy at birth
- Mortality Amenable to Health Care
- Hospital discharges for sepsis and wound dehiscence
- Disease Burden (Disability Adjusted Life Years)
- Diabetes lower extremity amputations
- Hospital admission rate for asthma, congestive heart failure, diabetes short term complications
- Trauma during vaginal delivery
- Cost-related access barriers
- Use of ER for non-emergencies
- Waiting times for primary/urgent care visits

Now let's look at some of the more positive aspects of what our primarily private healthcare programs have given us:

- Providing Treatment As Soon As Possible (ASAP) – With private health insurance programs your care is prioritized by your doctor. There are no lengthy queues and you can call your doctor anytime.
- You are Free to Choose Your Doctor – With private healthcare insurance you have a right to choose the physician(s) you wish with some caveats that will be discussed later. You can

---

[9] Gary Claxton, Cynthia Cox, Selena Gonzales, Rabah Kamal and Larry Levitt: Measuring the quality of healthcare in the U.S., 2015

also choose the most advanced equipment and services that can improve your chances of staying healthy.

- Better Facilities – Hospital and other facilities are generally state-of-the-art. Laboratory, patient support devices and services (renal dialysis for example) are readily available. Many patients in the United States are cared for in private rooms and if not in a private room, patients share a room with only one other patient. Most also have access to Wi-Fi, large room, television, good heat and air conditioning systems, and private (or semi-private) bathroom.

- More Relaxed Visiting Hours – When you are in a private hospital room, most hospitals relax visiting hours for those patients and oftentimes provide amenities for family members wishing extended, even overnight, stays with patients. Where systems utilize wards (rooms with 3 or more patients) patients' visitors can only come during specific hours.

- Proceeding without changes will mean special interests will continue to vigorously defend their turfs; we will have fractured health insurance programs as each state controls its own programs, and businesses and individuals will be caught in the middle. That will not be acceptable to most people.

- Moving forward in our attempts to improve our healthcare delivery programs (I purposely avoid using the word "system" because our healthcare delivery is too fragmented to be called a system) we will face many choices but each choice will generally fit into one of two options for the future. Those options are:

1. Work on improvements and additions to our existing programs – a mix of private insurance along with government programs Medicare for the elderly, Medicaid for the poor, CHIP for children, and the VA for veterans.

2. Move mainly toward a single-payer, socialized medicine program (something like that in the United Kingdom or Canada).

CHAPTER TWO

MAJOR ISSUES IMPACTING CHANGE DECISIONS

HEALTHCARE DELIVERY COSTS

Proceeding without changes will mean special interests will continue to vigorously defend their turfs; we will have fractured health insurance programs as each state controls its own programs, and businesses and individuals will be caught in the middle. That will not be acceptable to most people. This section is not an exhaustive review of all of the issues affecting the cost of delivering healthcare but is intended to touch briefly on some of the major issues. The primary purpose is to demonstrate that healthcare is extremely complex and there are no simple or easy solutions for the issues impacting all Americans.

ADMINISTRATIVE COSTS

It takes only a glance at a hospital bill or at the myriad choices you may have for healthcare coverage to get a sense of the bewildering complexity of healthcare financing in the United States. That complexity doesn't just exact a cognitive cost. It also comes with administrative costs that are largely hidden from view but that we all pay. Because they're not directly related to patient care, we rarely think about them.

A widely cited study published in The New England Journal of Medicine used data from 1999 to estimate that about 30 percent of American healthcare expenditures were the result of administration, about twice what it is in Canada. If that figure holds today, it means that out of the average of about $19,000 that U.S. workers and their employers pay for family coverage each year, $5,700 goes toward administrative costs.

Such costs aren't all bad. Some are tied up in things we may want, such as creating a quality improvement program. Others are for things we may dislike – for example, figuring out which of our claims to accept or reject or sending us bills. Others are necessary, like processing payments; hiring and managing doctors and other employees; or maintaining information systems.

That New England of Medicine study is still the only one on administrative costs that encompasses the entire health system. Many other more recent studies examine important portions of it; however, the story remains the same: Like the overall cost of the U.S. health system, its administrative cost alone is number 1 in the world.

Using data from 2010 and 2011, one study published in Health Affairs, compared hospital administrative costs in the United States with those in seven other places: Canada, England, Scotland, Wales, France, Germany and the Netherlands. At just over 25 percent of total spending on hospital care (or 1.4 percent of total United States economic output), American hospital administrative costs exceed those of all the other places. The Netherlands was second in hospital administrative costs: almost 20 percent of hospital spending and 0.8

percent of that country's GDP. At the low end were Canada and Scotland, which both spend about 12 percent of hospital expenditures on administration, or about half a percent of GDP.

Hospitals are not the only source of high administrative spending in the United States. Physician practices also devote a large proportion of revenue to administration. By one estimate, for every 10 physicians providing care, almost seven additional people are engaged in billing-related activities. It is no surprise then that a majority of American doctors say that generating bills and collecting payments is a major problem. Canadian practices spend only 27 percent of what the U.S. does on dealing with payers like Medicare or private insurers.

Another study in Health Affairs surveyed physicians and physician practice administrators about billing tasks. It found that doctors spend about three hours per week dealing with billing-related matters. For each doctor, a further 19 hours per week are spent by medical support workers. And 36 hours per week of administrators' time is consumed in this way. Added together, in 2006, administrative costs added an additional $68,000 per year per physician. Because these are administrative costs, that's above and beyond the cost associated with direct provision of medical care.

In JAMA (Journal of the American Medical Association), scholars from Harvard and Duke examined the billing-related costs in an academic medical center. Their study essentially followed bills through the system to see how much time different types of medical workers spent in generating and processing them. At the low end, such activities accounted for only 3 percent of revenue for surgical procedures, perhaps because surgery itself is so expensive. At the high end, 25 percent of emergency department visit revenue went toward billing costs. Primary care visits were in the middle, with billing functions accounting for 15 percent of revenue, or about $100,000 per year per primary care provider. This is because of the complexity of our system.

One source of complexity of American healthcare is its multiplicity of payers. A typical hospital has to contend with several public health programs, like Medicare and Medicaid, along with many private insurers, each with its own set of procedures and forms (whether electronic or paper) for billing and collecting payment. By one estimate, 80 percent of the billing-related costs in the United States are because of contending with this added complexity.

Another source of costs for healthcare providers is chasing patients for their portion of bills, the part not covered by insurance. With deductibles and co-payments on the rise, more patients are facing cost sharing that they may not be able to pay, possibly leading to rising costs for providers, or the collection agencies they work with, in trying to get them to do so. Using data from Athenahealth, the Harvard health economist Michael Chernew computed the portion of doctors' bills that were paid by patients. For relatively small bills, those under $75, 90 percent were paid within a year. For larger ones, those over $200, that rate fell to 67 percent.[10]

When I was at the hospital, collections were a problem. We used to say that when a person is sick or injured and comes to the hospital they would give anything to get better but once they are better, the hospital goes to the bottom of the list of those to be paid. I used to say that I understand some patients may not be able to afford to pay but I became a little less understanding after a memorable hospital experience.

It was circa 1990 that I received an envelope that contained a check for $70.00 along with a bill from 1932. Fortunately, the check had an address and phone number on it so I could call the woman who sent it. She explained that she had been in the hospital for 14 days, delivered a baby, and had a surgery. It was the middle of the depression and when she left the hospital she told the nun in the business office that she didn't have any money to pay the bill. She reported that the nun took her hand and said, "Honey, don't you worry about it. You go home and take care of that beautiful daughter and maybe, someday, you'll be able to pay us." The woman further explained that over the years as she would get an extra $70 she would

---

[10] Frakt, Austin: The Astonishingly High Administrative Costs of U.S. Health Care, The New York Times, July 16, 2018

think about paying the bill and then her daughter would need a coat and shoes, or someone would need medicine, or the water heater would go out, or they'd need tires for the car. Always something came up that prevented her from paying the bill.

She told me she had saved a little extra and had decided that rather than buying extra fuel oil for the winter, she was going to pay that hospital bill. I realized she still needed that $70.00 a lot more than the hospital did and I was about to tell her I'd like to return her check when she brought that thinking to an abrupt end. She told me that she had walked a few blocks to the mailbox, deposited the letter, and then hurried home, called her daughter and said, "Honey, you're mine now." I often wonder how we lost that sense of personal responsibility and think about how much better we would be if it permeated our society today.

The abovementioned administrative costs focus on dollars but there is a cost that cannot be easily translated into dollars. That is the physicians that retire early. I need to preface the following personal story by explaining that at the time we did not have a family physician. My wife went to an obstetrician, my children went to their pediatrician, and I had my healthcare needs met through my Air Force medical unit until my discharge a year or so earlier.

Following the birth of one of our children my wife developed blood clots in both of her legs (bilateral thrombophlebitis). She recovered fine but on December 23rd (a Friday) more than a year later she called me at work saying her right thigh was very painful, red, and swelled. My first thought was that she was having a recurrence of her thrombophlebitis and I told her to call her doctor immediately. She called her obstetrician and his response was, "That really isn't my thing to take care of, you need to call the doctor that took care of your blood clots when you had them before." That was understandable. She called the specialists that had taken care of her thrombophlebitis before and his response was, "I'm leaving on vacation so call back for an appointment after the first of the year." That was not understandable. She was in tears when she called me back asking me what to do. I went home and took her to the emergency department.

The E.R. doctor examined her, ordered some lab tests, an X-ray and determined that she did not have a blood clot. He then asked me who our family physician was so he could send his findings and the test results for follow-up. We were more fortunate than most would be in the same situation because I worked in hospital administration and knew many of the physicians that had hospital privileges. As I was thinking about who I should suggest for follow-up I saw a young family physician that was relatively new to our medical staff walking down the hall. I explained the situation to him and asked if he would take care of my family. His immediate response was, "Of course I will."

Later that evening, he called us at home to see how she was doing. He gave us a list of things to look for and said that if any of them occurred, call him immediately. It was a holiday weekend and he proceeded to give us a list of where he would be and the phone numbers where he could be reached. For the next 35 years or so he took care of me and my family. Then, during a visit for a routine exam, he announced he was retiring at the end of the month. He loved his patients and loved being their doctor but he had just had it. He was fed up with the hassle of the paper work and the increasing rules and regulations. Fed up with the time spent dealing with drug formularies (the drugs approved for payment by Medicare, Medicaid and insurance plans) and getting authorization for procedures. He just didn't enjoy practicing medicine anymore!

Fortunately, my wife and I found a wonderful primary care physician to continue the excellent care we had been receiving for many years. Unfortunately, as I write this book I have been told by our current physician that he will be leaving his primary care practice for a more fulfilling opportunity. He's leaving for reasons quite similar to the reasons our former physician retired early. Hope we can be fortunate to find another great primary care physician.

If we want to reduce administrative costs and continue to have provider and insurance choices, we must reduce administrative costs. This can only be accomplished by having a coordinated set of standards for pricing, billing and collections. Some steps toward reducing administrative costs include:

Standardizing Pre-Authorization Requirements – A typical insurer will have a multitude of policies regarding what findings must be documented before it will authorize further treatment. For example, an MRI and physical therapy might be required before orthopedic surgery. Some such requirements are natural and beneficial, but there are too many different requirements.

Integrating Medical Record and Billing Systems – Electronic medical records which record clinical information have no way to communicate information to payment systems run by insurers. Thus, when an insurer requires documentation of a particular diagnosis or prior treatment, it requires people to be involved. Contrast that to what happens when a person shops at Walmart. When an item is scanned at the register, the register automatically alerts the inventory system, which in turn automatically re-orders new inventory from the relevant supplier. The supplier's computer processes this information and arranges for new inventory to be sent to the store. All of this occurs without a single individual being involved. The goal should be the same in health care.[11]

Universal Form to Submit to Payors – Hospitals and other providers have to deal with multiple insurance companies not just from within their state but with insurance companies from all around the country.[12] We should be able to have a single form that is accepted by all payers be they government or private insurers.

---

[11] Carter, David M.: Reducing Health Care Costs: Decreasing Administrative Spending, Testimony for Senate Committee on Health, Education, Labor and Pensions, Hearing July 31, 2018

[12] White, Jess: Administrative costs climbing for hospitals, Healthcare News & Insights, January 22, 2015

PRIVATE HEALTH INSURANCE PRACTICES

My "beef" with insurance companies goes back to 1967. I remember that sometime around 1953 my father came home from work and, with a degree of pride even noticeable to a child, presented each member of the family with a health insurance identification card. He told each of us to carry it in our wallet or purse at all times because it assured that we would get the care we needed if we were sick or injured when away from home.

Between the time my father and his company began paying those insurance premiums and 1967, the insurance was used twice—once for my father's broken ankle (that he broke jumping to catch a football at a Boy Scout meeting) and for my appendectomy when I was 15. In March of 1967 my father was discharged from the hospital with a diagnosis of cancer, and within days he received a letter notifying him that his insurance had been cancelled. Insurance companies don't cancel plans that way today, but it is not because they care about the individuals they insure. It is because legislation was passed that forbids such cancellations.

You might think I would have learned from that experience that insurance companies are in business for the sole purpose of making money, but I didn't. I just became angry with that particular insurance company. I just thought it was them, not the entire industry.

It was 1995 when I was hit across the side of the head with a green two by four. I had resigned my position of vice president of a hospital with the intent of setting-up a consumer-driven healthcare insurance program that would right most of the wrongs that I had identified during my 30 years in the healthcare business. My first step was to go to insurance school so I could pass the test to be a licensed life and health insurance agent.

One of the first things the instructor said was, "We are not here to teach you insurance. We are here to teach you how to pass the test." That did bother me a little, but it was the second statement that struck me like a bolt of lightning. He said, "Now I'm going to give you the answer to a question that will most likely be on the test. The question is, "what is the purpose of an insurance company?" The answer, and never forget it, is to **make money!**"

I don't have anything against making money. I like to make money and businesses need to make money or they will cease to exist. However, for a small town boy, raised in a family that reached out to help those in need, and one who had spent 30 years working in a hospital founded on a mission and philosophy of helping others, the statement that insurance companies exist for the sole purpose of making money was sobering. It seems that any business should have a sense of obligation to their customers based on some moral/ethical value system—not just how much money we can make.

Let's get back to my sobering experiences with healthcare insurance. I was talking to a young man who told me he worked for a health insurance company. I asked him what he did and he told me his job was to find reasons not to pay claims. I told him I thought it was probably a pretty tough job to make sure that all of the charges on a healthcare statement were correct. He told me there were other people at the company to monitor that. His job, he said, was to scrutinize everything possible to find a "t" that wasn't crossed, an "i" that wasn't dotted or something that wasn't 100% correct on the application—anything at all that could be used as a reason not to pay any part of the bill. To me, the hiring of someone for the sole purpose of finding some minute reason not to pay a bill, just underscores that it is all about money.

Then, there is the insurance executive that I asked how frequently they denied a pre-certification for common surgical procedures and diagnostic tests like CAT and MRI. Pre-certification is the process whereby you or your physician calls the insurance company to get approval for high-cost diagnostic procedures, surgical procedures, and admission to a hospital, etc. I like to refer to it as your physician having to ask, "Mother, May I?" He told me that they don't deny very many at all. I asked him if they don't deny very many, why do they do it? He looked at me like I was the most naïve person in the world and said, "Because a lot of people don't ask, and if they don't ask, we can penalize them $500–$1,000 depending on the policy they have." It is all about money!

There is still more. Another health insurance company executive told me about their policy of always asking for additional information on any claim of $5,000 or more. He also told me that the bigger the claim, the more people they ask for additional information. He explained that on most cases they could request additional information from the patient, the hospital, and often times more than one of the physicians involved in the case. He told me that one reason they did it was to provide more time to find a reason not to pay the bill, but mostly it was to delay paying the bill. The longer they could delay paying the bill, the longer they could keep their money invested and the more money they could make. It is all about money!

All of that said, I have to acknowledge that insurance companies do have a fiscal responsibility to their shareholders and those they insure. If insurance companies just paid every bill that came through the door without question (especially hospital and surgery bills), then premiums would skyrocket, people would cancel their policies due to the high cost and the company would go out of business. However, there should be a reasonable balance between fiscal responsibility and doing what is "right" for the customer. My experience, however, is that the system today is highly biased toward finding reasons to deny or slow payments with little concern about the individual. It is all about money!

The question that logically follows is, why do we need, or want to keep, insurance companies involved in a national system? For one, the majority of Americans who have insurance obtain it through employer-sponsored or group health insurance plans. The coverage has numerous advantages – among them cost (including the government income tax exemption for health benefits), ease of enrollment, and a wide range of plan options. (In addition to a health insurance plan, employees may have the option to purchase insurance for dental, life, short- and long-term disability.)[13] In 2017, the sources of health insurance coverage for the total U.S. population were:[14]

Employer – 49% - 156,199,800
Non-Group - 7% - 20,525,500
Medicaid – 21% - 65,152,400
Medicare – 14% - 42,802,800
Other Public – 1% - 4,588,200
Uninsured – 9% - 27,753,700
*Total of 101% due to rounding

With all except 9 percent of our citizenry covered by health insurance, is it necessary, or wise, to disrupt the majority to help a few? Doesn't it make more sense to figure out how to serve the 9-10 percent (depending on the statistical bases used) and essentially leave the majority alone?

Private insurance subsidizes marginal to inadequate payments from government programs. For example, at Thomas Jefferson University Hospital, employer-sponsored health plans pay 636 percent more than Medicare for outpatient care, or non-urgent services that don't require being admitted to the hospital, according to a Rand report. Statewide, employer-sponsored health plans paid 144 percent more for outpatient hospital services compared with Medicare.

Rand researchers analyzed 2015-2017 data for about $13 billion in hospital spending from self-insured employers, state-based all-payer claims databases, and health plans in 25 states (New Jersey was not among the states studied). They compared negotiated rates for employer health plans with Medicare reimbursement rates for the same procedures and facilities. In Pennsylvania, most hospital claims data came from employers in the western part of the state. Researchers included hospitals if there were at least 11 claims from the employer plans that contributed data. As a result, a few Philadelphia-area

---

[13] Anderson, Steve: Private health insurance, health insurance.org, December 17, 2018

[14] Health Insurance Coverage of the Total Population: Kaiser Family Foundation, Timeframe of statistics, 2017

hospitals, including Jefferson and the Hospital of the University of Pennsylvania (where employers paid 233 percent more than Medicare for outpatient services) made it into the report.

The study was supported by the Robert Wood Johnson Foundation, the National Institute for Health Care Reform, the Health Foundation of Greater Indianapolis and employers who contributed their health plan data. Researchers found that in every state they studied, employer plans paid more for hospital services compared with Medicare — but how much more varied significantly by state. Employers in Michigan, for example, paid 56 percent more than Medicare for all hospital services (inpatient and outpatient), while their neighbors to the south in Indiana paid 211 percent more than Medicare. Hospitals say that Medicare underpays for services and that they are forced to negotiate higher rates with private plans to compensate. And Medicaid generally pays less than Medicare.

The Hospital and Healthsystem Association of Pennsylvania recently commissioned a study that found Medicaid pays hospitals about 81 percent of the cost of providing care to Medicaid beneficiaries, said Jeff Bechtel, senior vice president of health economics and policy for the association. He declined to provide a copy of the study. "Hospitals need to pay their bills and pay the 24-hour, seven-day-a-week services to individuals that depend on their care and because of the lower government payer rates, it's necessary and not surprising that rates for commercial payers are higher," Bechtel said.[15]

The cost shift from government programs to private programs does increase private health insurance premiums but it is largely this subsidy from private insurance plans that allow hospitals and doctors to have the resources necessary to provide quality and timely services and to bring new technologies to patients. Charging patients with the ability to pay a little more to subsidize the healthcare of the poor has been a part of healthcare for centuries. So has spreading the cost of expensive technologies across everyone so it is available to the few that

---

[15] Gantz, Sara: Private insurance plans pay hospitals far more than Medicare. Could price transparency fix that?, Philadelphia Media Network, May 9, 2019

need it. That said, there is a need to bring rationality to this subsidy system. This will be covered later.

To keep private health insurance plans as part of an integrated national health insurance program, it will be necessary to rationalize the interactions between individuals, providers and insurers. In addition to the suggestions in the administrative costs section there are some other steps worth considering.

Standardization of Insurance Application Forms – This would be especially helpful for those applying for individual or small group insurance plans. Simply fill out one electronic form and submit it simultaneously to multiple insurance companies. Competition is good!

Pre-certification and Case Management by Exception

Pre-certification is a system that forces physicians to ask, "Mother, May I?" Admittedly, there may be a few physicians that abuse the system, but my experience tells me they are a small minority. Let's stop running costs up by requiring all physicians to go through hoops and over hurdles to control a few. The system today is about like using a cannon to kill a gnat.

Pre-certification should be applied on an individual provider basis. Those that practice high quality, cost-effective medicine should not have to run an obstacle course to take care of their patients. Those that abuse the system, or just plain don't know any better, need the hoops and hurdles.

Establish Maximum Time for Adjudication of Claims and move toward Real-time Electronic Adjudication of Claims Linking an Identification Debit Card/Credit Card to the HSA and the Insurance Plan

An individual's insurance identification card can be a Medical Credit/Debit Card (MCDC) linked to the individual's Health Savings Account (HAS) and the insurer. The MCDC can be scanned at the physician's office, imaging center, laboratory, surgical center, pharmacy, hospital, etc. The amount authorized for the service being performed is displayed immediately and the healthcare service provider can explain to the patient the charges and how they compare with the approved amount.

The healthcare service provider is paid immediately through the MCDC with the charges going electronically to the patients HSA, and the insurer. The insurer credits the HSA with the appropriate payment, including any shared savings, and the HSA reduces the MCDC balance up to the amount in the HSA. If a balance remains, the patient would have the same options as they do with any other credit card. That is, pay it off when a statement is received or make monthly payments with interest accruing on the unpaid balance.

ABSENCE OF COST, CHARGE AND PRICE INFORMATION

A major factor in attempting to control increasing healthcare expenditures is that no one really knows what anything costs. Hospitals, physicians and other providers establish fee schedules also known as their charge master. However, charges have little, if anything, to do with cost. It is important not to make the mistake of equating "charges" with "price" or "cost." "Price" is the amount of money given and accepted for something of value – in other words, the amount accepted as payment for a service or item. "Charges," at least in healthcare, are the starting point for discount negotiations. "Cost" is the expenditure of money, time, labor, etc. to make something or provide a service.

I'll use my experience in the hospital clinical laboratory as an example of how charge and cost are not related. The hospital administrator (CEO) would come to me and say, "John, I need an additional $100,000 (sometimes the number was more, but never less than $100,000) from the lab next year. Increase your charges to generate it for me." What did I do? I would go to our data files that showed how many of each lab test we did during the past year. We had several hundred procedures but most of them didn't get ordered very often. Some, however, were ordered quite frequently—1,500 – 2,000 times a month for some tests like complete blood counts (CBCs), blood sugars, and urinalysis. Several others were ordered at the rate of 500 – 1,000 times each month. So, the easiest way to get $100,000 was to add one or two dollars to the charge for the high volume procedures to get $90,000–$95,000 of it, and then increase the charges for the low volume procedures enough to make up the difference.

The problem was, the actual cost for performing the high volume test was low, and the cost for performing the low volume test was high. The amount we charged for a test had very little to do with the cost of doing the test. This process was repeated throughout the hospital departments, X-ray, nursing service (daily room charge), surgery and all of the other revenue producing departments. It should also be noted that we had 40 or so departments in the hospital but only a handful produced revenue in excess of their operating expenses. These profitable departments included laboratory, X-ray, pharmacy, surgery, physical therapy, and nursing service. Those departments pretty much supported all of the other hospital services, including the increasing number of activities that were mandated by legislation and various regulatory bodies.

Next, there is no connection between charge and price. Here is an example of the hospital "discount game." It is an old example and reproduced from my 2008 book but the concept it represents is still valid. In February of 2007, my wife had rotator cuff surgery at a local hospital. It was same day surgery (also known as ambulatory surgery). She went into surgery in the morning and I took her home later in the afternoon. The total hospital "charges" were $22,205.81. The amount accepted by the hospital in payments from my insurance company and my co-payments (the "price") was $8,455.04. That is a discount of $13,750.77 or 61.9%.

About three months after my wife's surgery, the Chief Executive Officer of that hospital was a guest speaker at a service club I belong to. After his presentation that included comments about what the hospital is doing to contain costs, a member asked about the large discounts he sees on the Explanation of Benefits he receives from his insurance company. The CEO's response was, "You have a good insurance company that is working hard for you." Then the same member challenged the CEO further with a question about how much is paid by a person who is not insured and is paying his/her own bill. The CEO's response was, "Anyone who pays cash when they are discharged gets an automatic 20% discount." I was nice and kept my mouth shut but I do feel compelled to explore that answer in more detail.

Let's see. If you are an up-front, honest, hardworking individual who pays cash at the time of discharge, your $22,205.81 bill is discounted 20% or $4,441.16. That may sound good, but the reality is that you wind up paying a total of $17,764.65. That is $9,309.61 more than my insurance company and I paid and it took us three months to get the bills settled. Something is very wrong with this picture. It reminds me of grocery stores that require you to have "their card" to get "their discounts." I have never understood why they want to penalize me when I voluntarily choose to patronize their establishment but don't have "their card." It must work for them, but it doesn't work for me and I go out of my way to avoid them.

Okay, that example is from 2007 so let's look at one from August 2019. My wife is really a very healthy person and I don't want anyone to think otherwise just because I'm using her as an example again. It's just that I have all of the information on the case and it reinforces that things have not changed in the last 12 years. She developed an abscess in the middle of her back that did not respond to home treatments and grew to be quite large. Our family physician examined her and determined that it was beyond what he could do in his office and sent her to a surgeon to have it drained. He determined it was beyond what he could do in his office and sent her to the emergency department for the incision and drainage. During the four and a half hour process we interacted with 16 different individuals (all of whom were very friendly and competent) and the total charges were $7,007. The total paid including our copays was $1,150. That's $5,857 (84%) less than the charges. The EOB has a code that reads, "Charges in excess of Provider's fee schedule – DO NOT bill member for this amount. An uninsured person would be stuck with the full $7,007 in charges. Nothing has changed!

There has been an attempt to create some transparency for hospital charges. In the FY (Fiscal Year) 2015 IPPS/LTCH (Medicare Hospital Inpatient Prospective Payment System/Long-term Acute Care Prospective Payment System) proposed rule and final rule (79 FR 28169 and 79 FR 50146, respectively), CMS (Center for Medicare and Medicaid Services) noted that section 2718(e) of the Public Health Service Act, which was enacted as part of the Affordable Care Act, requires that each hospital operating within the United States, for each year, establish (and update) and make public (in accordance with guidelines developed by the Secretary) a list of the hospital's standard charges for items and services provided by the hospital. There are no hospitals operating within the United States with exemptions from this requirement under the current policy.

As shown in the examples above, publishing charges is almost meaningless. Unless hospitals and other providers share the amount they accept (the price or discounted charge) from insurers, just publishing charges to create transparency is an exercise in futility.

Go to DRG and CPT™ Pricing Structure

The only solution I have to propose to create transparency in hospital and other provider payments is to move all insurance companies and providers to DRG and CPT pricing.

There are over 500 Diagnostic Related Groups (DRGs) and all of the roughly 10,000 – 12,000 hospital diagnoses and procedures are placed in one of the diagnosis groups. The diagnoses are grouped by system (circulatory system, nervous system, etc.) according to resources needed to treat the problem. Each DRG has a payment rate associated with it and that rate is adjusted for the region of the country, city, etc. In other words, a DRG describes a diagnosis and treatment and has a price associated with it.

DRG pricing is based on averages. That means that someone who uses fewer resources than average, such as fewer days in the hospital, will pay for more than the cost of the services actually consumed.

On the other hand, someone who consumes more than the average will pay less than the cost of services consumed. This is something that businesses and individuals are going to have to get used to but it shouldn't be too hard since itemized bills won't be required with DRGs.

Average pricing has been used in the restaurant business for decades. As a teenager, one of my favorite family outings was to go to a smorgasbord. It was an all-you-can-eat dining room that had lots of things young growing boys liked to eat—meat, potatoes, gravy, and desserts. My parents especially liked it on Friday evenings when there were also large bowls of shrimp, lobster, and other fish dishes. The main point is that everyone paid the same price without regard to what they consumed. I'm certain that the restaurant lost money on me every time I walked through the door. I'm equally certain that they made money every time my mother or grandmother walked through the door. On average, however, people believed they were treated fairly, the restaurant made money, and you always knew before you walked through the door how much it was going to cost. Using average pricing for hospitals is also fair and should save money in the long run.[16] It also eliminates the billing mistake problems and the need to explain why the hospital might have charged $5 for an aspirin, a Band-Aid, or any of a number of other items that seem to carry excessive charges when viewed by a patient. Hospitals could easily post their DRG prices on line.

I'll use an admittedly oversimplified explanation of CPT™ codes to make my point. Basically, a Current Procedural Terminology (CPT™) code is somewhat analogous to a model number on an appliance or a part number on a repair part. The five digit number, sometimes with a modifier code added, describes a specific service. For example, Code 99213 describes a physician office visit of a defined duration and/or complexity, and a Code 82962 is a specific blood

---

[16] "Diagnosis Related Groups:" Duke University Medical Center, July 6, 1999. http://www.mcis.duke.edu/standards/termcode/drg.htm.

sugar test. There are more than 10,000 codes that describe the various healthcare services provided in physicians' offices, laboratories, X-ray units, surgery centers, physical & occupational therapy centers, and many of the services provided in hospitals. These codes are reviewed and updated on a regular basis by a panel of physicians nominated by the AMA (American Medical Association) and other healthcare organizations.

Posting the CPT™ Code and the associated accepted payment (price) will help to open the door to price competition among providers. There is one issue with this though - CPT™ is a registered trademark of the American Medical Association and negotiations may be required for purposes of publishing pricing information.

THE UNINSURED

If we are to address the problem of the 9-10 percent of our citizenry being uninsured we must first understand what causes them to be uninsured. The Affordable Care Act (ACA) led to historic gains in health insurance coverage by extending Medicaid coverage to many low-income individuals and providing marketplace subsidies for individuals below 400% of poverty. The number of uninsured nonelderly Americans decreased from over 44 million in 2013 to just below 27 million in 2016. However, in 2017, the number of uninsured people increased by nearly 700,000 people.

Even under the ACA, many uninsured people cite the high cost of insurance as the main reason they lack coverage. In 2017, 45% of uninsured adults said that they remain uninsured because the cost of coverage is too high. Many people do not have access to coverage through a job, and some people, particularly poor adults in states that did not expand Medicaid, remain ineligible for financial assistance for coverage. Other reasons for being uninsured among uninsured nonelderly adults are:

Lost job – 22%

Lost Medicaid – 11%

Status change* – 11%

*marital status change, death of spouse or parent, ineligible due to age or leaving school

Employer does not offer or ineligible for coverage – 9%

No need for health coverage – 2%

Most remaining uninsured people are in working families, are in families with low incomes, and are nonelderly adults.[17]

I am going to include Unauthorized Immigrants in the uninsured category. The unauthorized resident immigrant population is defined as all foreign-born non-citizens who are not legal residents. Most unauthorized residents either entered the United States without inspection (sometimes referred to as illegal or unlawful) or were admitted temporarily (student or work visa) and stayed past the date they were required to leave. The number of those overstaying their visa is generally estimated at 40-45 percent of the unauthorized immigrant population. Unauthorized immigrants are neither eligible for Medicaid nor to buy insurance. Lawful immigrants under 400% of poverty are eligible for tax credits to purchase coverage and after five years may become eligible for Medicaid.

The number of unauthorized immigrants is a fuzzy number based on old data at best and I have not seen any reports that represent to me anything more than a SWAG (Scientific Wild Ass Guess). However, the number most frequently used today is about 12 million. With solid up to date data from all sources being essentially nonexistent, it is impossible to accurately assess the dollar amount these people place on nationwide healthcare expenditures. One writer estimates it to be $18.5 billion[18] but it could be much higher than that. What we'll examine here is how are healthcare services for the unauthorized immigrants delivered and paid for.

States can use state-only funded Medicaid programs to cover services for unauthorized immigrants. California for example uses

[17] Key Facts about the Uninsured Population: Kaiser Family Foundation, December 7, 2018

[18] Conover, Chris: How American Citizens Finance $18.5 Billion in Health Care For Unauthorized Immigrants, The Apothecary, February 26, 2018

such funds to cover all children regardless of immigration status through their Medi-Cal program. Other states including New York, Illinois, and Washington have similar programs.

The Emergency Treatment and Active Labor Act requires that hospitals treat emergency patients regardless of their ability to pay. Hospitals that serve large numbers of uninsured patients (disproportionate share hospitals) receive some subsidies from Medicare and Medicaid to help offset the cost of those services.

Federally qualified community health centers provide primary healthcare, dental, mental health and pharmacy services to all without regard to immigration status or ability to pay. Additionally, physicians provide a significant amount of charity care.

So, the question is, "What should the United States government do to provide more healthcare for the uninsured?" As harsh as this may be, I propose only limited expansion of federal programs above and beyond the subsidies already in place. I also believe that legislation to increase those subsidies must be passed by a super majority of both the House and Senate to preclude small majorities of the same political party from forcing programs down the throats of all Americans. Nowhere in the Constitution is there an obligation for the federal government to provide healthcare. Although we can all agree that all persons, regardless of status, are entitled to basic healthcare, the obligation for providing those services should rest at the state level. States can expand their programs to include any residents they want to include. They can implement programs for those who have lost their insurance for any reason or length of time they choose. If a state cannot afford to cover the costs of providing healthcare to the unauthorized immigrants of their state, they can assist federal immigration authorities in identifying and deporting those that do not have a legal right to be in the country. If a state decides to be a sanctuary state or to allow sanctuary cities, that is the choice of the residents of that state. The individual states and their residents should be financially responsible for their decisions. The one exception to this is mental health. Mental health is a major national issue that needs to be addressed but I believe it should be outside of our existing programs. More about that later.

DRUG ABUSE

The following statistics are from the American Addiction Centers:[19]

- According to the National Survey on Drug Use and Health (NSDUH), 19.7 million American adults (aged 12 and older) battled a substance use disorder in 2017.
- Almost 74% of adults suffering from a substance use disorder in 2017 struggled with an alcohol use disorder.
- About 38% of adults in 2017 battled an illicit drug use disorder.
- That same year, 1 out of every 8 adults struggled with both alcohol and drug use disorders simultaneously.
- In 2017, 8.5 million American adults suffered from both a mental health disorder and a substance use disorder, or co-occurring disorders.
- The most common types of prescription drugs abused in 2017 were pain relievers, tranquilizers, stimulants, and sedatives. In 2017, about 1.7 million people age 12 and older had a pain reliever use disorder.
- In 2017, an estimated 14.5 million American adults age 12 and older battled an alcohol use disorder and more than 10 percent of U.S. children live with a parent with alcohol problems.
- Drug use and addiction cost American society more than $740 billion annually in lost workplace productivity, healthcare expenses, and crime-related costs.
- There are many causes of addiction including genetics, chaotic home environment, abuse, peer influences, community

---

[19] Addiction Statistics Reviewed by Scot Thomas, M.D.: American Addiction Center, May 13, 2019

attitudes toward drugs, poor academic achievement, and mental health disorders.

- In 2017, an estimated 20.7 million people age 12 and older needed treatment for a substance use disorder. Only 4 million people received treatment, or about 19% of those who needed it. Of the more than 18 million people who needed but did not receive treatment for substance use, only 1 million of those people felt they needed treatment.

Now that we have an overview of the addiction statistics, we need to address why people become addicted and some approaches to attacking the problem.

Experts say that when you break it down, addiction is a mental disorder – a compulsive engagement with something that makes you feel rewarded or happy, despite the fact that the experience can bring unfavorable consequences.[20]

Addiction is due 50% to genetic predisposition and the other 50% to poor coping skills. Children of addicts are 8 times more likely to develop an addiction.[21] Simply put, genetics can be something parents, grandparents or great-parents have passed down through generations.[20] However, genetics do not make you an addict; they do make it easier to become one once your experiment with drug to which you have a predisposition for addiction. Addiction to one substance increases the chances of addiction to another. We may not be able to change our genetics, but understanding our family history can help us to avoid triggering a predisposition.

Coping skills are those daily strategies and activities that we use as people to help deal with, work through, or process our emotions. We all have them. We have learned them from our families and the people who influenced us most in our lives.[22]

Early in life, people may develop methods of managing stress that will hinder the ability to cope with situations appropriately,

---

[20] Barnes, Shayler R.; Health (www.news4jax.com), May 20, 2019

[21] Addictions and Recovery: April 12, 2019

[22] Ernest, Chad, MS, LPC: Sunny Sky Counseling, September 4, 2014

according to "Psychology Today." Low coping skills may cause a person problems in relationships and work. A lack of coping skills in many occurs during childhood and can play out through adulthood or may be a result of a traumatic experience that occurred in a person's past.[23]

We live in a society today that hinders the development of coping skills. Children often participate in activities in which everyone wins – no one loses. Everyone gets a trophy! Even young children know that there are other children that are faster, stronger, taller, and more athletic. Some are more musically or academically talented. How can people learn to cope with defeat if they are not allowed to lose? We now have safe spaces to protect people from others that think differently than they do. Why did we permit colleges and universities to shelter students from hearing and discussing opposing views? How can graduates compete in the workplace if they have not learned to listen to others, and calmly and knowledgably discuss and debate, and then win or lose gracefully?

In the United States there are more than 14,500 specialized treatment facilities providing counseling, behavioral therapy, medication, case management, and other types of services to persons with substance abuse disorders. Physicians, mental health clinics, counselors, psychiatrists, psychologists, nurses and social workers are additional sources of help.[24] Major issues that need to be addressed are the stigma associated with treatment and the lack of parity for insurance coverage of mental health and substance abuse programs.

What is of grave concern to me is the lack of a national focus on development of coping and social skills in children. We have to start by addressing the disintegration of the family and a society chaos.

Constitutionally we are a country of laws; however, we don't have to look very far to see that in many instances we do not walk the talk. We say we are committed to taking care of our veterans but 38,000

[23] Scheidies, Cassandra: Reasons Why People Have Low Coping Skills, Healthfully, July 27, 2017
[24] Principles of Drug Addiction Treatment: A Research-Based Guide (Third Edition): National Institute on Drug Abuse

remain homeless[25] and the Veterans Administration estimates 20 veterans take their own lives each day.[26] We do little to improve our services to veterans. President Trump's Mission Act (allows veterans to use private healthcare providers in certain cases) is under attack while cities and states are allowed to become sanctuaries for the millions of people in our country illegally as they refuse to work with federal agencies like Immigration and Customs Enforcement (ICE). There seems to be at minimum four sets of laws - one for politicians, one for the rich and well-connected, one for illegal aliens and one for the rest of us.

The top priority for most our politicians seems to be to get elected and re-elected. They say what they think people want to hear so they get the vote, but once elected they vote whatever the party bosses and/ or lobbyists tell them to vote. How are people supposed to cope with the most powerful people in the country caring more about funding for an upcoming election than they are about the people they were elected to represent? Candidates are donor-driven and we, the people, allow ourselves to be bullied by propaganda. How do you cope when people you admire and respect turn out to be sleazy and dishonest?[27] Fixing a society in chaos begins with fixing politics in chaos. Term limits may be a good place to start.

Biologically we are born male or female and there are physical differences – not just in reproductive rolls but physically and emotionally. Males have larger hearts, greater lung capacity and more muscle than females yet transgender males are allowed to compete against females in sporting events. A male can decide that he identifies as female and is allowed to use female restrooms and locker rooms. Political correctness and the desire to be all things to all people are destroying our social structure. There really are differences between boys and girls, men and women.

[25] Shane III, Leo: Veterans, Fewer veterans were homeless in 2018, Veterans, November 1, 2018

[26] Kirst, Sean: Memorial Day, veteran suicides and a moment of hope, The Buffalo News, May 26, 2019

[27] Paraphrased from Tucker Carlson Tonight: May 29, 2019

While I was managing a hospital clinical laboratory one of my best female supervisors came into my office and announced that she was resigning immediately. After talking with her for about 45 minutes the truth came out. She was upset because a new female employee had for weeks been hanging her coat on the coat hook the supervisor had been using for many years. I asked her if she had talked to the new person about it and she had not. Fortunately we were able to quickly resolve the issue. Had the same issue occurred between men I'd be willing to bet that the male supervisor would have quickly made it clear to the new male employee which coat hook he could use. Men and women often times do have different emotional reactions to events. This is not to say the differences are either good or bad, most likely a little of each. However, the differences do exits. As a society we should strive for equality between genders while recognizing that there really are differences.

How many times does history have to repeat itself before we learn that values matter? Families matter. Moral courage matters. Honor and integrity matter - not only for individual happiness and prosperity, but for the good and strengthening of society. Which fails us first - The family or society? What messages do infanticide and gender related abortion send to our children and to the outside world? Too many parents become distracted by all that society is offering, and they fail to focus time and instruction toward their children. Children, having no guidance because of absent parents, become swayed by what society is offering, the cycle continues, and compounds with each new generation.[28]

According to the United States Census Bureau, 23 percent of children live with a single mother. During the 1960-2016 period, the percentage of children living with only their mother nearly tripled from 8 to 23 percent and the percentage of children living with only their father increased from 1 to 4 percent.

We also have to address the impact of social media. We are more connected today than ever but reliance on social media can have a

---

[28] Allison, Rachel: Cause and Effect: Family Disintegration and Society Chaos

negative effect on our mental health. We all have our fair share of insecurities, some that we speak about openly and others that we prefer to keep to ourselves.

As human beings, it is important to communicate and forge personal connections with each other. This is hard to do when we are glued to the screen becoming more familiar with our friend's digital facades than their real life persona.

Not only has social media been proven to cause unhappiness, it can also lead to the development of mental health issues like anxiety or depression. I think about how different it is for children today. When I was in school, if I was having a problem with a fellow student, when school was out, I could go home and be away from the problem until the next school day. I had time to think about it and sometimes ask advice from my parents or a sibling. Not so today. With social media, children can be bullied 24/7 and the impact that can have on self-esteem is incalculable. Children are more unhappy and depressed today than ever before.[29] At minimum we must start restricting the amount of time children are allowed to spend on social media and maximize the time they spend in face-to-face communication.

Drug abuse and addiction are only going to get worse unless we declare a war on the causes. We have made good progress after declaring war on cigarettes, cancer, and CO_2 emissions. We can slow the growth of illegal immigrants. We can clean up our streets from those using them as toilets and places to buy, sell and use drugs. We can control our children's use of social media and their participation in extremely violent video games. We can emphasize the importance of families. We can work to de-stigmatize mental health counseling. We can clamp down on the smuggling and sale of illegal drugs. We can get our politicians to focus more on the country than on themselves if by no other means than limiting their terms. Seats in the House and Senate were never intended to be full time positions.

---

[29] Center for Discovery: November 9, 2016

PHARMACEUTICAL INDUSTRY

Colorado has capped the price of co-pays for insulin, making it the first state to enact a law that combats the soaring costs for the medication that have doubled in the last seven years.[30] The article continues to say that insulin prices have reached $1,000 a month on average and that high prices have led some diabetics to forgo the medication or ration doses, putting their lives at risk. How can a pharmaceutical that's been around since 1923 cost so much?

It's All About Money! However, some do care about mankind.

Doctors Frederick Banting, Charles Best and James Collip were awarded a patent in January 1923 for their method of making insulin. When they were ready to turn over the patent of their discovery to the University of Toronto for production purposes in 1923, they agreed to receive only $1 each (the equivalent of $14 today) in compensation. The patent was necessary to restrict manufacture of insulin to reputable pharmaceutical houses who could guarantee the purity and potency of their products. It would also prevent unscrupulous drug manufacturers from making or patenting an impotent or weakened version of this potentially dangerous drug and calling it insulin.[31]

Since insulin was in such high demand, the university granted Lilly (and other pharmaceutical companies) the right to make it, royalty free, and also offered them the ability to improve the original formulation and patent anything they developed down the road. **It was all done for the benefit of mankind** at that point but it opened the door to big profit-chasing and the business of diabetes was born shortly thereafter.[31]

A Chicago Daily Tribune story from April 1, 1941, reports that a federal grand jury indicted a corporate trio – insulin manufacturer

[30] Ellis, Nicquel Terry: Colorado sets limit on co-pays for insulin, USA TODAY, May 25, 2019

[31] Hoskins, Mike: Way Back When...Insulin Was Cheap (And Then It Wasn't), healthline, September 28, 2016

Eli Lilly in Indianapolis, distributor Sharp & Dohme in Philadelphia, and drug maker and distributor E.R. Squibb & Sons in New York – for conspiring to unlawfully "bring about arbitrary, uniform, and non-competitive prices for insulin and to prevent normal competition in the sale of the drug." All three companies eventually pleaded "no contest" but never admitted any wrongdoing. Newspapers reported that the accused companies were fined $5,000 each and their corporate officers each faced $1,500 in individual fines for the price-fixing charges.

Insulin prices (and the prices of many pharmaceuticals) have always been an issue for folks with marginal incomes but costs became a factor when insurance companies started using co-pays for prescriptions and newer insulins and delivery systems became available circa 2000. It's too bad we can't take a step back into the past when insulin was considered a resource for the public good rather than a product ripe for a high-growth billion-dollar market.[31] My guess is that pharmaceutical companies will continue to tweak various insulins to keep them under patent and prevent the manufacture of generics that could reduce prices dramatically.

This is not intended to be an exhaustive dissertation about the increasing cost of prescription drugs, but it wouldn't be fair to leave readers thinking insulin manufacturers are the only drug companies holding people hostage by aggressively increasing the price for brand name drugs. Take Martin Shkreli, the former chief executive officer of a little known company, Turing Pharmaceuticals. He bought the rights to a drug, Daraprim, that was invented before he was born and raised the price from $13.50 to $750 a pill. Daraprim is a drug often used by patients with HIV.[32] The pill still costs $750 and there is still no generic version.

I have to acknowledge that there have been tremendous advances in healthcare due to new drugs. HIV is no longer a death sentence, organ transplants are commonplace and many cancers are being

---

[32] Johnson, Carolyn: What happened to the $750 pill that catapulted Martin Shkreli to infamy, The Washington Post, August 1, 2017

effectively treated. But it is projected that the total spending on medicines will reach $1.5 trillion by 2021.[33] With that much money at stake and in the absence of pharmaceutical leadership guided by moral and ethical standards, we must demand more transparency in the industry.

Nothing in the pharmaceutical industry is transparent and an August 2016 Gallup Poll found that no industry is held in lower esteem by U.S. citizens than pharmaceuticals[34] - its rating is even lower than the federal government. "Drugs are tested by the people who manufacture them, in poorly designed trials, on hopelessly small numbers of weird, unrepresentative patients, and analyzed using techniques that are flawed by design, in such a way that they exaggerate the benefits of treatments. Unsurprisingly, these trials tend to produce results that favour the manufacturer. When trials throw up results that companies don't like, they are perfectly entitled to hide them from doctors and patients, so we only ever see a distorted picture of any drug's true effects. Regulators see most of the trial data, but only from early on in a drug's life, and even then they don't give this data to doctors or patients, or even to other parts of government. This distorted evidence is then communicated and applied in a distorted fashion. In their 40 years of practice after leaving medical school, doctors hear about what works ad hoc, from sales reps, colleagues and journals. But those colleagues can be in the pay of drug companies – often undisclosed – and the journals are too. And so are the patient groups. And finally, academic papers, which everyone thinks of as objective, are often covertly planned and written by people who work directly for the companies, without disclosure. Aside from all this, for several of the most important and enduring problems in medicine, we have no idea what the best treatment is, because it's not in anyone's financial interest to conduct any trials at all. These are ongoing problems, and although people have claimed

---

[33] Van Arnum, Patricia: The Top 10 Issues for the Pharma Industry in 2017, DCAT Value Chain Insights, January 18, 2017

[34] De Felice, Damiano: How Pharma Can Fix Its Reputation and Its Business at the Same Time, Harvard Business Publishing, February 3, 2017

to fix many of them, for the most part they have failed; so all of these programs persist, but worse than ever, because now people can just pretend that everything is fine after all."[35]

Then we have the issues of how much it actually costs for a pharmaceutical company to bring a new drug to market. The cost to bring a medicine from invention to the pharmacy shelf is estimated by Tufts Center for the Study of Drug Development at $2.7 billion while an article published in JAMA (Journal of the American Medical Association) Internal Medicine sets the cost at $648 million.[36] So, which is right? Possibly both, depending upon the pharmaceutical company, the number of drugs the company researches and develops, type of drug being developed, and what is included in the cost. If the analysis includes only the costs of research, clinical trials, etc. for a specific drug, the $640 million figure could be about right. About 9 out of 10 drugs fail to make it to market because at some stage of the process they are proven either not effective or not safe. Including the cost of failures in the analysis pushes the cost over the $2 billion mark. Additionally, some companies track the effectiveness of the drug for several years and include those expenses when they report the cost of drug development. Bottom line, there is not a universally accepted method of determining the cost of bringing a new drug to marker, but regardless of the method utilized to determine cost, bringing a new medicine to the market is expensive.

Pharmaceutical companies, like all other companies, have to make a profit! The only reason people invest in a company is to make money. If a company doesn't have a profit, it doesn't have money to develop new or improved products and it cannot give a reasonable return on investment to its investors. The question then is how much is a reasonable profit for a product that impacts the lives of almost everyone and is life extending or life saving for many? Research data on 99 cancer drugs shows that by the end of 2017, the

---

[35] Goldacre, Ben: Bad Pharma: How drug companies mislead doctors and harm patients, 2012

[36] Herper, Matthew: The Cost of Developing Drugs Is Insane. That Pater That Says Otherwise Is Insanely Bad, Harpers, October 16, 2017

median cumulative sales income was $14.50 per dollar invested for research and development. The median time to fully recover the maximum possible risk-adjusted cost of research and development ($2.8 billion) was five years. Cancer drugs continue to generate billion-dollar returns for the originator companies. Lowering prices of cancer drugs and facilitating greater competition are essential for improving patient access, health system's financial sustainability, and future innovation.[37]

The next issue with drug pricing is with the pharmacy benefits managers (PBMs). Pharmacy benefit managers serve as intermediaries between the insurance plan sponsor and pharmacies. They determine which pharmacies will be in the plan's network, develop the formulary (list of covered medications), and negotiate price rebates with drug manufacturers. Manufacturers provide these rebates in exchange for having specific medications listed on the formulary.[38] PBMs drive up drug prices and interfere with patients' access to medications.[39] Sometimes the copay a patient pays for a prescription is more than the insurance company pays for the drug. The difference goes back to the PBM. This is called a clawback. Clawbacks (think kickbacks) to PBMs should go toward reducing the cost of drugs for the patient.

In the fall of 2018 I was prescribed a medicine to treat actinic keratosis (AK) which is a growth on the skin considered precancerous because if left untreated, it can develop into skin cancer. AK occurs on areas of the skin after years of exposure to the sun. Since this drug was not on my insurance plans formulary, I had to pay the full cost out of pocket and it wasn't inexpensive. Fortunately, I was able to do

---

[37] Tay-Teo, Kiu, PhD, Ilbawi, Andre, MD, Hill, Suzanne R., PhD: Comparison of Sales Income and Research and Development Costs for FDA-Approved Cancer Drugs Sold by Originator Drug Companies, JAMA Network Open, January 4, 2019

[38] Hoey, B. Douglas: Rebates to pharmacy benefit managers are a hidden contributor to high drug prices, STAT, November 28, 2016

[39] Wapner, Jessica: UNDERSTANDING THE HIDDEN VILLAIN OF BIG PHARMA: PHARMACY BENEFIT MANAGERS, Sign In, March 17, 2017, Published in Newsweek June 3, 2019

so but there are many who could not afford to do so. A little side note here. Always use sun screen and teach your children to use sun screen beginning at a very early age.

Here is an industry idiosyncrasy I just discovered. I'm on Medicare and currently pay $98 per month for a supplement plan. For several years I've taken enalapril maleate and hydrochlorothiazide for high blood pressure. When I started the medication I was taking one 20 milligram enalapril tablet and one 12.5 milligram hydrochlorothiazide capsule per day and my copay for a 90 day supply was $0.00. Over time I lost 60 pounds and the hydrochlorothiazide was eliminated and my dose of enalapril was reduced to 10 milligrams and then to 5 milligrams. Since I had a supply of 20 milligram tablets I just cut the tablets in half for the 10 milligrams and then into quarters for 5 milligrams. When I told my doctor I had about exhausted my 20 milligram tablets I asked him to just write me a new prescription for 5 milligram tablets. He has all of my insurance information on his computer screen and when he was entering the prescription he said, "Your insurance plan doesn't like a 5 milligram prescription. It likes 2.5, 10 and 20 but it won't pay for 5." He wrote the prescription for 5 milligrams anyway but told me to ask the pharmacist what their retail price is because sometimes for generics the insurance copay is more than the retail price. When I picked up my prescription the charge was $18. It isn't the $18 cost that bothers me. It is that my insurance will pay if I have a prescription for 2.5 milligrams, 10 milligrams, or 20 milligrams but won't pay the 5 milligrams that I actually need. You would think that since high blood pressure can contribute to stroke, heart attack and kidney disease that it would be in the best interest of the insurance company (and certainly the patient) to cover such a low cost medication. That doesn't make any sense at all. By the way, the pharmacist I use tells me their computer system always defaults to generics if available unless otherwise requested by the physician or patient. If the retail is lower than the copay, they automatically drop the charge to the retail price and they do not participate in clawbacks. I'm not convinced that clawbacks to PBMs don't occur somewhere along the line but I can't prove it so I'll just remain a skeptic.

So, how do we fix the industry if it is fixable? I think there is only one answer – *Transparency*! Pharmaceutical companies spend billions marketing their drugs directly to consumers as well as to physicians. It's hard to watch a television show without seeing advertisements for drugs. So let's start there. Drug advertisements should include the list price of the drug along with the list of possible side effects they currently include (oftentimes in small print). This can spur competition and might dissuade some people from demanding a prescription for a drug that their physician doesn't think they need.

We can take this one step further. Pharmacies should post the list price for the 15-25 most common prescription drugs and have the prices readily available for those drugs not posted. Additionally, they should share the typical amount paid by insurance plans. Let's make it so everyone pays the typical negotiated price.

OVERUSE OF TECHNOLOGY

There is a lot of technology available to healthcare providers but how much of it is overused and do we always know everything we should know before using it? Even though it is not related directly to healthcare, an experience from my childhood may help to exemplify what I mean. I remember going to the shoe store and when trying on different shoes I would be told to stand in a shoe-fitting fluoroscope and I could see how my shoes fit. It was pretty neat to look down through that tube and see the bones of my feet inside the shoes. It was a new marketing tool that blasted our feet with radiation. Not well established knowledge at the time, if it was actually even known, that the radiation presented risks for the bone development of children if overused.

Regarding how much is really known about a technology before it is placed into routine use I offer the following. As of this writing, I have found information on 10 open medical device class action lawsuits. These are: Hernia Mesh lawsuit, Bone Cement lawsuit, Essure Birth Control lawsuit, Stryker Hip Implant lawsuit, Depuy

Elbow Implant lawsuit, Neurovascular Stents Lawsuit, Depuy Attune Knee Implant lawsuit, IVC Filters lawsuit, Bair Hugger lawsuit, and Transvaginal Mesh lawsuit.[40] As in the pharmaceutical industry, transparency of the investigative process might either prevent a device from going on the market or at minimum provide the patient with full disclosure of all risks before agreeing to the procedure.

Current estimates for unnecessary expenditures on overuse range from 10 to 30 percent of total health care spending.[41] By some estimates, overuse of health care services amounts to $780 billion annually. One example is vertebroplasty, a procedure for patients with spinal fractures that involves injecting cement into the spine. Insurers in the U.K. and Australia stopped paying for it in 2009 because it was conclusively shown to have no net positive value and a lot of complicating side effects for patients. The U.S. still performs about 80,000 such procedures a year! There are dozens of examples like this.[42]

Then there is the CT (Computed Tomography) scan. The use of CT scans in the United States grew from 3 million in 1980 to more than 85 million in 2011. Although CT scans are an essential diagnostic tool, the Food and Drug Administration reports that an estimated 30-50 percent of imaging tests are believed to be medically unnecessary.[43] Studies published in 2007 and 2009 by teams from Columbia University and the National Cancer Institute predicted that up to 2 percent of future cancers – about 29,000 cases and 15,000 deaths annually – might be caused by CT scans.[42] The cumulative effect of radiation exposure is especially of concern in children who undergo 5-9 million CT scans annually.

---

[40] Classaction.com: June 6, 2019

[41] Brownlee, Shannon: Saini, Vikas; Cassel, Christine; When Less Is More: Issues Of Overuse In Health Care, Health Affairs, April 25, 2014

[42] Elshaug, Adam, PhD: Combating Overuse and Underuse in Health Care, The Commonwealth Fund, February 23, 2017

[43] Goodman, Sandra G.: Heavy Use Of CT Scans Raises Concerns About Patients' Exposure to Radiation, Kaiser Health News, January 6, 2016

My interest in the CT scan was piqued when my daughter shared a hospital bill she received for an appendectomy performed in the spring of 2019 on my 21 year old grandson. The total charge was an astronomical $53, 986.53 and included a CT scan priced at $2,535. When I saw that charge the first that came to my mind was how incredibly absurd the charge was. We know there is no relationship between cost and charge in healthcare and that insurance companies don't pay the full charges, but there are some poor souls that are going to have to pay the full charge. An August 7, 2018 report on Howmuchisit.org shows the average charge for an abdominal CT scan to be $590. The senseless and illogical charge of $2,535 is shameless and immoral. Understanding that the CT scan may be the best radiological modality for diagnosing appendicitis, I do question the need for it in his case because he was exhibiting so many indicators of appendicitis.

The Alvarado score is a clinical scoring system used to evaluate the risk of appendicitis in patients presenting with abdominal pain. It assigns points to eight factors including elevated temperature, elevated white blood cell count, tenderness in the right lower quadrant of the abdomen, etc. A score of 5 or 6 recommends observation and repeat examination of the patient while a 9 or 10 is very probable appendicitis and recommends surgical intervention.[44] My grandson had a score of 9. Was his CT scan medically necessary? Was it defensive medicine? Was it because it is a cash cow? Maybe some of each but my suspicion is that it was a little defensive medicine and a lot cash cow.

It appears the same situation applies to the use of Magnetic Resonance Imaging (MRI). One study found that for MRI of the lumbar spine only 443 of 1,000 requests were considered appropriate. The remainder were split between inappropriate (285 of 1,000[28.5%] or of uncertain value (272 of 1,000 [27.2%]. On the positive side,

---

[44] Shogilev, Daniel J., MD, Duus, Nicolaj, MD, Odom, Stephen R., MD, Shapiro, Nathan I., MD, MPH: Diagnosing Appendicitis: Evidence-Based Review of the Diagnostic Approach in 2014, West Journal Emergency Medicine, October 7, 2014

82.8% of MRI request for headache were considered appropriate.[45] Are those not considered appropriate the result of defensive medicine or the pleasant sound of a cash register ringing?

The cost of defensive medicine (use of tests/procedures used solely for the purpose of avoiding lawsuits) is nearly impossible to get a good handle on. I have found estimates of annual spending on defensive medicine that range from $35 billion to $850 billion. However, I know that doctors and hospitals want to avoid lawsuits so I think the $35 billion figure is low to say the least. Gallop reports that one in four healthcare dollars can be attributed to defensive medicine – about $650 billion annually. Despite tort reforms, 90% of doctors in Massachusetts and 77% in Texas said they have not changed their practice of defensive medicine.[46]

The extra costs associated with defensive medicine could be mitigated using a Patient Compensation System (PCS). Under a PCS, physicians and hospitals would no longer be sued for medical malpractice. Instead, hearings would be held in front of a panel of healthcare experts. If the panel finds that a medical injury was preventable, the patient would receive compensation. Another approach might be a loser pays system. If you bring a lawsuit and lose, you pay all costs including the defendant's legal expenses. Frivolous lawsuits would drop dramatically.

Removing the financial incentives to overuse technology can be overcome by using a capitated payment system like the DRG and CPT systems used by Medicare. Physicians and hospitals cannot survive on the rates paid by Medicare so reimbursement would need to be a few percentage points higher but the impact would be the same. It forces the providers to closely monitor utilization to keep their costs as low as possible.

---

[45] Emery DJ, Shojania KG, Forster AJ, Mojaverian N, Feasby TE: Overuse of Magnetic Resonance Imaging. *JAMA Intern Med.* 2013;173(9):823–825. doi:10.1001/jamainternmed.2013.3804

[46] Scherz, Hal, MD, Oliver, Wayne: Defensive Medicine: A Cure Worse Than The Disease, Forbes, August 27, 2013

INDIVIDUAL RESPONSIBILITY

Dennis Prager said, "Most people do not yearn to be free. Most people yearn to be taken care of."[47]

When writing about Mr. Prager's comment, Brooke Medina made an important distinction between the freedom that men, women, and children from war-torn parts of the world are dying to achieve. She explained that the freedom Prager is referring to is more akin to duty, such as the duty of behaving like an adult when it is more tempting to relegate those grown-up responsibilities to someone else.

In all likelihood, you and your vested interests are part of the problem too. If you have never questioned or challenged a charge for a healthcare service you received, never questioned your physician regarding the necessity of a test, procedure or medication he/she recommended, never "shopped for price" for healthcare services, and never demanded quality information from healthcare service providers—then you are part of the problem.

Several years ago my son had an accident in which he received a large cut on his arm. He went to a hospital emergency department and was fixed-up with more than 100 stitches. He was visiting home a couple of weeks later and he asked me to look at his bill to see if it seemed reasonable since it was for more than $5,000 and he thought that might be a little high.

After looking at the bill, I asked him if he had any heart problems while in the ER, if he had been on a heart monitor, had lots of lab work done, and had a heart catheterization. He said no to the heart monitor and lab tests but asked how he would know if a heart catheterization had been done. I told him they would have made an incision in his groin area and run a tube about the size of a speedometer cable through his artery into his heart. He admitted to being a little shaken-up over the accident but said he certainly would have known if they had shoved a speedometer cable up his leg, and they didn't.

---

[47] Prager, Dennis: Conservative Leadership Conference, April 13, 2018

He called the hospital; they reviewed the records, and discovered that charges for a heart patient had been mistakenly charged to his account. They corrected the mistake quickly and all was well. The most disconcerting thing was that when he contacted his insurance company and informed them of the mistake, they had already processed the claim and had to retrieve the check before it went in the mail. It does reinforce the fact that patients need to question anything that does not make sense to them.

It is also very easy for a hospital to charge patients and their insurance companies for mistakes the hospital makes. One retired hospital CEO told me that mistakes made in nursing service (giving a wrong medication, transfusing the wrong blood, etc.) really bothered him because they can lead to lawsuits. But he thought performing the wrong lab test or X-raying the wrong leg, however, is okay. Those kinds of mistakes don't hurt anyone, you just do them over again, and the great thing is you get to charge for both.

The point of both of these examples is that patients need to get itemized bills and review every charge for mistakes. I have not done a survey to determine how many people scrutinize the list of items and the prices when they check out of a grocery or department store but I know my wife is a hawk at it. What is amazing is that 50 percent or more of the time she finds mistakes and most of them involve items that were on "special" but the "special" price had not been entered into the computer system. Same thing can happen at healthcare facilities where tens of thousands of items and procedures have a price tag.

If you expect your healthcare insurance plan to pay for all of the healthcare you want (there is a big difference between "want" and "need"), if you go to your physician every time you get a sniffle because "it only costs a $5 or $10 co-pay," if you use the emergency room for care that could be provided by your primary care physician, if you think it is up to the government alone to "fix" the healthcare problems, if you complain vehemently when your employer passes some of the healthcare insurance cost increase on to you, or if you think you should be able to consume all of the healthcare services you want at someone else's expense—then you are part of the problem.

For the most part, individuals have been sheltered from the true cost of healthcare. Their employer pays most of the insurance premium; the individual has low deductibles, low co-payments, and low coinsurance. As a result, the perception is that healthcare is free, or at least almost free. The individual has little reason to care about how much healthcare services cost or how many of them are consumed. I have heard many individuals say, "It only costs $5.00 for me to go to the doctor. I go to mine for everything, even if I know I really don't need to be seen." In short, people tend to want on-demand, gold-plated, Cadillac medicine at someone else's expense. Such a consumer attitude works counter to most attempts to control healthcare costs.

If you are overweight, smoke, and don't exercise, if you abuse drugs, if you do not have regular check-ups and don't control your blood pressure, cholesterol, and blood sugar, if you think you have the right to abuse your health and have your excesses paid for by someone else, or if you don't have mammograms, pap smears, and colonoscopies as recommended—then you are part of the problem.

Most individuals have contributed to the high cost of healthcare most likely because they just want to be taken care of, are sheltered from the costs, and/or have not made the effort to learn what they can do to contribute to solving the problems. If we are to gain control of healthcare costs while assuring access to quality services, then the grown-up responsibilities associated with these goals cannot be relegated to someone else.

MENTAL HEALTH

Mental health is a very delicate issue and as the British might say, somewhat of a sticky wicket. According to MentalHealth.org, "mental health includes our emotional, psychological, and social well-being. It affects how we think, feel, and act. Many factors contribute to mental health problems, including: Biological factors, such as genes or brain chemistry; life experiences, such as trauma or abuse; and family history of mental health problems." Following are some of the feeling or behaviors listed as early warning signs of mental health problems: Eating or sleeping too much or too little; having low or no energy; having unexplained aches and pains; feeling helpless or hopeless; smoking, drinking, or using drugs more than usual; feeling unusually confused, forgetful, on edge, angry, upset, worried or scared; having persistent thoughts and memories you can't get out of your head. There are others but these are enough to make my point – is there anyone who at some point, or points in their life, has not experienced many of these warning signs?

I don't make the point to demean those individuals that have serious, long term mental health issues. I make it to demonstrate mental health issues can be very complex and sometimes hard to recognize when a problem might be a short term situational issue that will pass or is more serious requiring intervention. People with serious mental health issues may not recognize the problem themselves and may lack the close family or personal relationships to steer them to the needed help.

A 2019 report by the National Alliance on Mental Health (NAMI) includes the following:

- Approximately 1 in 5 adults in the U.S. (46.6 million) experience mental illness in a given year with 1 in 25 (11.2 million) experiencing a serious mental illness.
- Approximately 1 in 5 youth aged 13-18 (21.4%) experience a severe mental disorder at some point during their life and for children aged 8-15 the estimate is 13%.
- 2.6% of adults in the U.S. live with bipolar disorder; 6.9% of adults (16 million) had at least one major depressive episode in the past year.
- 18.1% of adults in the U.S. experienced an anxiety disorder such as post traumatic stress disorder, obsessive-compulsive disorder and specific phobias.

The same NAMI report lists the following social statistics:

- An estimated 26% of homeless adults staying in shelter live with serious mental illnesses.
- Approximately 20% of state prisoners and 21% of local jail prisoners have "a recent history" of a mental condition.
- 70% of youth in juvenile justice systems have at least one mental health condition.
- Only 41% of adults in the U.S. with a mental health condition received mental health services in the past year.
- Half of all chronic mental illness begins by age 14 and three-quarters by age 24.

Approximately 800,000 children are reported in the foster care system nationwide at any one time and 40-85 percent have mental health problems.[48] There are 8 common reasons children enter the foster system: Abuse, Neglect, Illness, Incarceration, Death, Drug abuse, Child's choice, and Voluntary placement.[49] How can any of these children not have a mental health problem?

One of the things that make mental health problems so difficult to identify and treat is that they are not always obvious to either the individual or those close to him. It is not like a heart attack – the individual knows it and those observing the incident know something is wrong. You break your leg you most likely know it right away and those around you see that you're not walking right. Most mental health problems are not intuitively obvious, somewhat like high blood pressure. The difference is that high blood pressure is easily diagnosed and quickly treated (if you are seen by your doctor on a regular basis). Not so with mental illness.

When I started in healthcare in 1965 our community had a shortage of mental health practitioners and it wasn't just a problem

[48] Carter, Rosalynn: Solving the Mental Health Crisis for Our Children, Life the Blog, November 17, 2011

[49] Harmon, Amy: 8 Big Reasons Kids Enter the Foster Care System, adoption. com, May 17, 2016

in our community – it was a nationwide problem. I don't have data on the number of providers from 50 years ago but my guess is that the situation has not improved. According to the American Journal of Preventive Medicine, in 2018 the number of behavioral health practitioners per 100,000 people are: 15.6 Psychiatrists, 30.0 Psychologists, and 2.1 Psychiatric NPs. This is not very many considering the population with mental health issues.

Counties Should Take the Lead

Counties run 91% of local jails and invest $70 billion in community health systems like behavioral health services each year.[50] County leadership is the closest to all aspects of the problem and is in the best position to solve their specific issues. The federal government cannot solve the problem primarily because of the tendency for them to create one size fits all policies. If there is a need for additional federal funding for mental health services that should come in the form of block grants to the states.

POLITICS

Last but not least in my abbreviated list of major issues impacting the decisions we have to make as part of the healthcare debate is politics. The United States is a heterogeneous society and does not have a set of widely accepted cultural norms. This makes some conflict inevitable. Division on subjects such as immigration, race, gender identity, environment, energy, abortion (from conception through infanticide), rules for transgendered individuals, assisted suicide, reparations, "free" higher education, and single payer healthcare may have the country nearly as divided today as it was during the Civil War. I experienced the great division during the Vietnam Conflict but I don't think it was nearly as bad then as it is today. During

---

[50] Cox, Greg: Counties Are Key to Solving Our Nation's Mental Health Crisis, Commentary, StepUpTogether.org, May 16, 2019

Vietnam, the division was primarily focused on one issue – Vietnam. Today we are surrounded by division on nearly every subject and we've reached the point where it is rare to find people who can have a quiet, fact based discussion of their differing opinions. What should be discussions turn into shouting matches, name calling, hate speech and all too often violence. All of this division is exacerbated by the absence of objective reporting and "journalism" based on political ideology rather than honest analysis of all available information and data. Although it would be ideal to facilitate reasonable compromises on all of the above, that's not my purpose here. My interest now is to focus on attempting to find an acceptable solution to the divisions surrounding healthcare.

First, let's look at the major areas of conflict. I think they can be simplified to four basic issues:

1. People want to be kept healthy, get better when they are sick, and feel better about themselves when they don't like something about their body, all without personal responsibility and at someone else's expense.
2. Doctors want to practice good medicine but they are hampered by rules, regulations, paperwork, concern about lawsuits, and large workloads necessitated by marginal payment systems.
3. The government(s) and people want more medical care for less money.
4. Healthcare businesses (hospitals, pharmaceutical manufacturers, healthcare professionals, medical device manufacturers, insurance companies, trial lawyers, etc.) want to make more money.

Unfortunately, trying to create a Utopian healthcare system, where everything is perfect for everyone, is not realistic – at least not now nor in the foreseeable future. So I'll try to keep this as simple as possible and take things one step at a time. Let's start with Dr. Robert Pearl's analysis of what patients and physicians really want from healthcare.[51] Focus group participants were asked to rank 22 healthcare attributes as either most important, of moderate value or of minimum value. At the top of the list for patients were doctor-patient relationships, evidence-based medical treatment and care coordination. Access and facilities were seen as offering moderate value, with the least importance assigned to technology and preventive services. Physicians were asked to do the same ranking and the top three results were the same. Physicians added preventive services to the category of offering moderate value but relegated technology and facilities to least important.

Based on Dr. Pearl's analysis, I'm taking people wanting everything at someone else's expense out of the equation. That's essentially special interest politics and it isn't realistically attainable. We should be able to agree that everyone in America should have basic and lifesaving medical care. Funding of additional community health clinics can give individuals access to basic primary care where relationships can be formed and preventive services provided. This should dramatically reduce the use of hospital emergency departments as primary care providers.

Reducing paperwork by addressing administrative costs, as mentioned previously, can go a long way toward reducing the non-productive time that consumes enormous amounts of a physician's time but individuals need to get involved with reducing healthcare expenditures and in recognizing the full cost of services. Some of this has been previously noted and it will be addressed in more detail later. More difficult from a political standpoint is the need to draw some lines of demarcation between what insurance companies and the government pay for and what costs are the responsibility of the individual. I'll use two examples that I'm sure will bring strong negative reactions. One is breast implants, implant removal and reconstructive surgery. There needs to be a standard set of thresholds used by all payers. The second is sex reassignment treatment and

---

[51] Pearl, Robert M.D.; What Patients And Physicians Really Want From Healthcare (Spoiler: It's Nearly The Same), Forbes, June 8, 2017

surgery. I know there are psychologists that believe an individual's physical appearance should match their emotional identities but I believe those changes should be the responsibility of the individual not society as a whole. Little Persons (dwarfism) have tremendous physical and emotional struggles and have a few not-for-profit support groups but as a society we do little to help them. I suspect that most people have some emotional identity of something they are not. After all, I have the emotional identity of a world class professional golfer but neither my body nor skills match that identity. Should society pay for my body building and skills training to bring me closer to an emotional identity match? I don't think so. As new knowledge and technology emerge, special interest groups will be lobbying for more and more treatments and procedures that walk the line between need and want. At this time, I think such decisions are best handled at the state level through votes of the people, not national political representatives, to determine what they are willing to pay for. Above all, we must eliminate the idea that society must pay to "fix me" when I am dissatisfied with what my parents' genes and God gave me.

I firmly believe we need to have up and down votes by the people on many of these issues. Unfortunately, I don't think we can trust our politicians. My experience tells me that most of those seeking political office promise what they think people want to hear to get voted into office but have very sub-standard performance on delivering those promises. Much of the problem is that once elected, the focus turns to raising money for the next election and most of that money comes from special interest groups. Pharmaceutical manufacturers, trial lawyers, unions, insurance companies, Planned Parenthood and the LGBTQ community are among the most powerful and well-funded. A Patient Compensation System or a Loser Pays system are suggested as possible solutions to the trial lawyer issue.

When writing my first book I met with a U.S. Congressional Representative to explain my consumer-driven pilot program and seek his assistance in obtaining a waiver to include some individuals enrolled in Medicare and Medicaid in the pilot. After explaining the program he said that it sounded great but I was wasting my time talking to him. He explained it this way:

First, he said, it is not our job (Congress) to help people like you solve problems.

Second, if I did try to help you, whatever I proposed would have to go through the Senate healthcare committee. Since your program is not a government controlled, single-payer system, the senator controlling that committee (Ted Kennedy) would not allow it to the floor for consideration.

Third, your program is a long-term solution to the problem and elected officials do not support long-term solutions. If your program cannot produce results in a time frame that will get votes the next time someone is up for election, few are going to support it.

Along with needing short-term solutions that will help them get re-elected, politicians need to respect the oftentimes conflicting positions of their campaign supporters and powerful lobbies. Healthcare organizations, pharmaceutical manufacturers, and insurance companies are powerful, well-funded, and are driven by their own bottom lines. In essence, I believe the best solutions to the healthcare problems in this country are such political "hot potatoes" that few politicians are willing to take them on.

Regarding our politicians and special interests I only have one recommendation - Term Limits! Our founders never envisioned political office as a lifetime career and they were right. I think Harry S. Truman had it right when he said, "Term limits would cure both senility and seniority – both terrible legislative diseases." Remember, for businesses, it is all about money, and for politicians it is all about votes!

─── **CHAPTER THREE** ───

SINGLE-PAYER
HEALTHCARE

As I begin this chapter I have to admit up-front that I am biased against single payer healthcare systems. I do recognize that there are many appealing aspects of the single payer systems used in the United Kingdom and Canada but I am not yet convinced that is the best direction for the United States. I do, however, try very hard to keep an open mind and willingly listen to those wanting to change my mind. Before going into details about the pros and cons of single payer systems, I will share the three experiences that led to my bias.

The first was in the early 1970s when I was serving as a medic in an Air Force medical reserve unit. A surgeon in the unit had just completed a year of residency in the United Kingdom and among the things he shared was a story about a man he had done back surgery on. He explained that this man had been at home on disability for three years waiting for his turn to get the needed surgery. In addition the surgeon also told me he had been working with a physician that had been a resident for 12 years. That resident told him that he would be applying for a new surgical position just authorized by the health ministry but he didn't think he would get it because he knew of 5 surgeons who had been residents longer than he.

The second occurred in the early 1990s. A woman from England was visiting our community while her husband was giving some guest lectures at Purdue University. She called asking if she could have a tour of our hospital so she could compare our hospital with the one in her home town. As we toured she shared that she was so happy that just before leaving for America she had received a call from a friend saying they had finally raised the money needed to buy a CT scanner for their hospital. The health ministry would not authorize one for their hospital so the community initiated a fund raising campaign to buy one. Following the tour I walked her to her car and as she started to open the car door she turned to me, took my hand, looked back at the hospital and said, "Everything here is so much bigger, better, and brighter – fight like hell to keep it that way."

The third was also in the early 1990s. A local businessman called to ask if I could give a nurse from a socialized medicine country a tour of the hospital. She was in town to be with her husband who was receiving a graduate degree from Purdue. Our hospital was licensed for 365 beds and the one she worked at was 450 beds. As we went through areas like the CT and MRI scanners I'd ask if she had that technology at her hospital and would answer that they did not but the services were available at the university hospital about 70 miles away. When we walked through the renal dialysis unit she asked me, "who in your country is eligible for dialysis?" I responded that everyone is and asked if that was not the case in her country. She said, "No, no one over the age 57 can have dialysis, unless of course if they are rich and can afford private treatments." I then asked her if someone went on dialysis at age 55 could they continue after age 57. She was obviously disturbed by the question and as she turned her eyes away she said, "No! I repeat, no one age 57 or older gets dialysis. Their treatments are discontinued."

Now that I have that off of my chest and you understand my bias, we'll dive into some of the pros and cons of single payer systems.

THE BASICS

In its most basic form, a single payer healthcare system is one in which every citizen is enrolled in the same insurance program, the cost is covered by taxes, and all of the services and payments are controlled by the government. Everyone has the same coverage – no one gets more and no one gets less. It is a one-size-fits-all program. From a socialist perspective this may seem like Utopia. Despite Utopia being an imaginary place, there are some beneficial realities to single payer healthcare.

THE PROS[52,53]

Everyone gets covered. This may be the most attractive element of a single payer system. The surgeon I wrote about earlier that operated on a man who had been on a waiting list for three years said that when he was telling me about his experience in the United Kingdom. There is no discrimination on any basis for citizens of the country.

Providers are paid at the same rate. No more does one provider (doctor, hospital, etc.) take less in payment for someone that is insured and more from someone that is not insured.

It creates spending leverage. The large, single pool of money provides strong negotiating power for pharmaceuticals, medical devices, etc.

No bills and reduced paperwork. Individuals don't receive bills for services and, depending on the system, may or may not have co-pays. The amount of paperwork is greatly reduced.

Health insurance costs go away. Taxes will be higher but people don't pay insurance premiums.

---

[52] Ayres, Crystal: 15 Pros and Cons of Single Payer Health Care, Vittana Personal Finance Blog.org

[53] British Healthcare System Pros and Cons List: NYLN Youth Leader Blog, August 6, 2016

THE CONS[52,53]

Some single payer systems allow for a private-pay option. In this case, many medical providers may opt for private pay only patients since poor pay under single payer only is not very attractive. This would likely reduce the number of options for people in the single payer system.

It does not solve the doctor shortage problem. Forbes reported in 2016 that even with the growth of specialists there will be a shortage of 94,700 doctors in the U.S. by 2015.

The money has to come from somewhere. Although health insurance premiums may go away, the costs of providing the care do not. Employers and individuals will pay for these services through taxes be they corporate taxes, withholding taxes, sales tax or some other form of taxation. Nothing is free!

Long wait times for specialized services. The wait times cited in my example from the early 1970s may no longer exist but wait times for non-emergency services of 6-8 months or more are common in the United Kingdom and Canada. What comes next – rationing based on an assessment of the value of someone's remaining life or social status? I fear that is the dangerous slippery slope of single payer.

The size of government increases. This increase will mostly be non-elected career bureaucrats that will control the system but have little to no incentive to be responsive to needs for change.

Less incentive to innovate. When everyone gets paid the same amount, there is little incentive to innovate or work on improving the efficiency or quality of the services.

Lack of Choice. In single payer systems patients have limited, if any, choice of doctors, hospitals or other providers. Consumer choice is a driver of innovation, improving efficiencies, and improving quality in most sectors of the economy – without it, all of them slow down or disappear completely.

In short, I think single payer healthcare is deceptive like a watermelon – nice and green on the outside but very red on the inside.

CHAPTER FOUR

WHERE FROM HERE?

To me, the most attractive pros of a single-payer system are that everyone is covered and the administrative paperwork is reduced. As attractive as those are, I think we need to explore ways of developing a system that incorporates them while avoiding, or at least minimizing, the cons.

I could go on nearly ad infinitum with comparisons of U.S. healthcare to various single-payer systems with things like population distributions, the numbers of CT, MRI, and PET scanners, joint replacement surgeries, organ transplants, etc. per 100,000 people. I'm not going to do that because it would bore you with numbers that would be out of date before this book is published and I don't think it would add to my objective of defining strategies to reach the goal of a hybrid healthcare system that combines the best of single-payer and private healthcare. For those of you that want to explore all of those statistics just hop on the internet. The footnotes and some of the other documents I've consulted when writing this publication are listed in the back of the book. They will give you a good start on your exploratory journey.

COMPETITION DRIVEN BY PRICE, QUALITY AND SERVICE—NOT NETWORKS

*This is directly from my 2008 book, "It's All About Money: Winning the Healthcare War" so although the charges used are much lower than they would be today the principles exemplified still apply today.

To appreciate the problems with networks and the problems they've helped create, you need to understand where they came from. At least through the late 1960s and into the early 1970s, my perception is that things were pretty good from the hospital and physician perspectives. People almost deified physicians, and hospitals were the nucleus around which most sophisticated healthcare services orbited. Patients rarely questioned what their physician told them, they didn't ask much except fairly superficial questions, they pretty much did what their physicians told them to do, and only the bravest of the brave would seek a second opinion.

The hospitals were up there on a pretty high pedestal too. Beds were full, patients stayed in the hospital for a long time (average length-of-stay was in the 7-8 day range as I recall); it was not uncommon to have a waiting list of patients to be admitted, and pretty much anything that could not be done in a physician's office, was done at the hospital. Times were good. The money flowed in and patients didn't even have to be treated as though they were people. Patients were often referred to as a room and bed number like 319A, or an organ or procedure like "the gallbladder" or "the appendectomy" in bed 418A. There were also a lot of rules and philosophies that were akin to cruel and unusual punishment for patients and their loved ones, but that is another book.

Then, all of a sudden, the world started to change and pedestals began to crumble. There were more physicians, and patients became more demanding. Physicians started doing laboratory studies in their offices, taking lab work away from hospitals. Physicians opened urgent care centers, removing paying patients from hospital emergency departments. Physicians opened outpatient surgery centers and started competing with hospitals for surgery business. Having been employed at a hospital during those times, I think I have a sense of how stagecoach lines, livery stable owners and blacksmiths must have felt as trains and automobiles replaced the horse as the primary means of transportation. It was somewhat like being in the path of a tornado and not having a storm cellar.

Let's examine some of the major factors that spawned the tornado and look at the vicious, upward-spiraling funnel that lifted the roof off of the healthcare house. By understanding a little about the storm, we should be better prepared to design a plan to bring things back down to earth.

First, we need to recognize that affordable, accessible healthcare for all Americans have been an issue for decades. Theodore Roosevelt included the need for a national health service in the 1912 platform of the Bull Moose Party (Progressive Party)[54] when he ran for president. Despite nearly a hundred years of rhetoric, we have never developed a healthcare system in the United States. We have a few hundred thousand independent businesses (physicians, hospitals, pharmacies, etc.) competing for a limited supply of customers (patients).

Although it was probably not recognized at the time, President Kennedy seeded the tornado when he proclaimed in 1961 that America would place a man on the moon and return him safely to earth before the end of the decade. Billions of dollars were pumped into the space program. As I analyze it, those billions brought new and improved technology to healthcare: telemetry to monitor the vital signs of the astronauts while in flight; faster, lighter computers to process the massive amounts of data required for space flight; fiber optics to transmit more information and transmit it faster using

---

[54] "Platform of the Progressive Party." August 7, 1912.

lighter weight materials. All of this, and more, was developed using federal funds and the developments were in the public domain.

By the early to middle 1970s, new medical technology was beginning to hit the market place. CAT scanners began to appear in hospitals. Medical uses were found for ultrasound technology. Reliable, economical, automated laboratory equipment was developed that made it profitable (and more efficient and convenient) for physicians to do lab tests in their offices. Microsurgical techniques, MRI, arthroscopy and more and more technology flooded the market making it practical to do more and more outside of the hospital setting.

Another big event occurred in 1965 with the legislation to implement Medicare coverage for senior citizens and Medicaid coverage for the financially indigent. Although the programs were, and are, well intentioned, the cost projections were so far below the actual costs that reductions in payments began almost immediately. The promise to pay providers their cost plus a small margin never materialized. The result has been a major cost-shift to the private sector. If the real cost for providing a service (personnel time, equipment, materials, etc.) is $1,000, and Medicare only pays $900, the additional $100 to cover the costs is added to the bills of the commercially and privately insured patients.

Now the stage is set. Medicare and Medicaid don't pay enough to cover costs, so charges to those who do pay have to be increased. This is where many hospitals made a huge mistake in the 1970s. I'll use my experience in the hospital clinical laboratory as an example. I am repeating this from Chapter Two because the concept is important and there I used it in a somewhat different context.

The hospital administrator (CEO) would come to me and say, "John, I need an additional $100,000 (sometimes the number was more, but never less than $100,000) from the lab next year. Increase your charges to generate it for me." What did I do? I would go to our data files that showed how many of each lab test we did during the past year. We had several hundred procedures but most of them didn't get ordered very often. Some, however, were ordered quite frequently—1,500 – 2,000 times a month for some tests like complete blood counts (CBCs), blood sugars, and urinalysis. Several others were ordered at the rate of 500 – 1,000 times each month. So, the easiest way to get $100,000 was to add one or two dollars to the charge for the high volume procedures to get $90,000–$95,000 of it, and then increase the charges for the low volume procedures enough to make up the difference.

The problem was, the actual cost for performing the high volume test was low, and the cost for performing the low volume test was high. The amount we charged for a test had very little to do with the cost of doing the test. This process was repeated throughout the hospital departments, X-ray, nursing service (daily room charge), surgery and all of the other revenue producing departments. It should also be noted that we had 40 or so departments in the hospital but only a handful produced revenue in excess of their operating expenses. These profitable departments included laboratory, X-ray, pharmacy, surgery, physical therapy, and nursing service. Those departments pretty much supported all of the other hospital services, including the increasing number of activities that were mandated by legislation and various regulatory bodies.

Well, you've probably already figured out what happened. Charges for the low cost, high volume procedures got very high relative to the cost of doing them. It didn't take long for the entrepreneurs to figure out that with all of the new technology, they could set up laboratories, X-ray services, physical therapy departments, surgery centers, etc. and charge less than the hospitals and make a lot of money in the process. The tornado had started sucking the not-so-sick, high volume, low cost patients and procedures out of the hospital into alternative settings. The more patients that were sucked out of the hospitals, the more hospitals had to increase charges to cover the costs for the Medicare and Medicaid patients, the poor patients who couldn't pay, and the very high cost services like trauma care in the emergency department, cardiac and medical/surgical intensive care, burn care, neonatal intensive care, cancer care, etc. It became a vicious upward spiral.

To try to keep hospital beds full and protect their business, hospitals and physicians started competing for patients. First, with what I call the pure public relations, mushy, feel good ads that said things like, "...caring for our community for more than 100 years...," and "...it's our CARING that makes us different!" Unfortunately, there is still a lot of money being spent on that kind of baloney. Don't take me wrong. I am not against advertising by hospitals, physicians, and other healthcare providers. It is just that I think the advertising should convey something substantive. Presenting information and data about quality is one example of something substantive.

Then the competition moved to the financial side. The trouble is the competition was structured to "steer" patients toward the physicians and hospitals. In short, the insurance companies and large self-insured businesses said to the physicians and hospitals, "You give us a discount, and we will provide incentives for our patients to use your services." Consumer choice just took a giant step backwards.

Before I address networks, however, I feel compelled to say a couple of things in defense of hospitals. Since their inception, hospitals have taken on the mission of providing care for all who present themselves for service without regard to ability to pay. They have been the healthcare safety net catching everything that came their way. The primary focus of hospitals was to take care of patients, and whether charges had any reasonable relationship to costs of specific services, was secondary. A personal example may help to clarify the picture.

As mentioned in Chapter Two, my father was diagnosed with terminal cancer in 1967. When he was dismissed from the hospital following this diagnosis, his insurance company cancelled his coverage (granted, that cannot be done today, but the story helps explain some of the thinking in hospitals at the time). My father was referred for Cobalt (radiation) therapy. My family was of modest means and the out-of-pocket expense for this treatment was of great concern to my mother. I asked the radiation oncologist how much this would cost and he told me the treatments would run $200–$300. I asked him how many treatments there would be and he indicated he wouldn't know until he examined my father, but it would be a series of several treatments.

I guessed there would be 10 -12 treatments, did some quick math and told him that we'd figure out some way to come up with the $2,000 or so to pay for the treatments. His response was, "No, I said $200–$300. That will be the total cost." I told him that I knew the cost of the equipment, how much it cost to replace a Cobalt source, the cost of personnel, and that I thought the $200–$300 was the charge for each treatment.

He explained that the charge was not based on the cost of providing the service. He said that it was very common for insurance companies to cancel coverage when patients were diagnosed with cancer, and that by the time the patient was referred for radiation therapy, the cost was a big issue for many families. He further explained that for many patients, the radiation treatments were not curative, but only palliative—they relieved pain and improved the quality of life for at least some of the time that the patient had remaining. He went on to say that rather than have any patient go without whatever benefits the treatments had, they just charged a small amount and covered the actual costs by adding 50 cents or a dollar to common procedures like chest X-rays. Whether it was right or wrong to use that approach for financing high cost, low volume procedures can certainly be debated; however, the humanitarian motive behind the approach was pure.

There were also anti-trust and many other regulatory issues that prevented hospitals from responding differently to the market forces. The point is, hospitals may have made some mistakes, but there were many factors involved, and, we have to remember that hindsight is always 20/20. Now, let's get on with righting the ship.

Networks are identified in several ways. Preferred Provider Organizations (PPOs) may be the most frequently used term. Physician Hospital Organizations (PHOs) are less common. However, there are Other Weird Arrangements (OWAs) galore (I'd like to credit the originator of the wonderful term OWA, but I have not been able to identify who used the term first). It really does not make much difference what you call them, they are all pretty much the same and they have run their course. I'll just refer to all of them as networks.

Networks are not very complicated. A person, an organization, a group of organizations, or an insurance company decides to develop a network of physicians, hospitals, and/or other healthcare providers. They then meet with the healthcare providers they want in the network (in reality, they don't often limit themselves to those that they really want; they'll talk to pretty much anyone who will listen). They offer the healthcare providers the promise of patients in exchange for discounts. This arrangement sounds reasonable in that there are economies of scale in healthcare just as there are in most businesses.

There are at least four major problems, however. First, and this may be because I am a little old fashioned, I don't think anyone, or any entity, should tell a person which physician or hospital s/he should use simply because of a discount. For most of my 20 years in hospital administration, one of my duties was contract management. I was involved in many network contract discussions and not one single discussion included any quality-of-care issues—only discounts! There were not even discussions regarding the initial price or the final price. The thinking was that the higher the initial price and the higher the discount, the larger the perceived savings for their customers.

Second, networks add an expensive administrative layer. Typically, the physician or hospital sends a bill to the insurance company. The insurance company sends the bill to the network to apply the negotiated discount. The network returns the adjusted charge to the insurance company that then processes the claim, sends checks to the physician and hospital, and informs the individual how much the insurance company has paid and how much of the bill is the responsibility of the individual. The network gets its money either in the form of a per-member-per-month network access fee paid as part of the insurance premium or as an additional discount from the physician or hospital—sometimes they get a little of each. There is one business in my geographic area that at one time paid $12.00 per member per month to access discounts. That is an extreme example and most access fees are much less.

Third, the days are gone when the network strictly limited the physician groups or hospitals included in the network. As a result, they provide very little steerage and are not very effective in increasing the number of patients delivered to the network providers. In the early days of networks, they frequently offered exclusive contracts that did provide strong steerage. Over time, however, many gave in to the pressure from consumers for more choice. Basically, almost all physicians and hospitals are in one or more networks and they are primarily giving discounts so they won't be excluded from the plan. Everyone, except the networks of course, would be better off if the discount games were eliminated and charges to all purchasers decreased to more closely reflect the cost of providing the service.

Fourth, and an egregious and most disconcerting problem, is that your network may have a discount, but a discount from what? From September 1995 through July of 1997, the employees of 70 businesses voluntarily submitted the Explanation of Benefits (EOBs) that they received from their insurance companies to us for analysis. We analyzed more than 10,000 EOBs during that time and the results were astounding. For a very common physician's office visit (CPT Code 99213) the charges ranged from $20–$78. The most frequent (prevailing) charge was $49. The prevailing discount was 15% (range 5%–20%). Therefore, the amount paid by most insurance companies and their patients was $49 minus 15%, or $42.00 (we round everything to the nearest dollar).

This is where things get disturbing. The physician that had a retail charge of $78 gave a 20% discount to a network resulting in a network price of $62. If patients who were covered by an insurance plan using that network went to an out-of-network physician who only charged the prevailing rate of $49, the patients were penalized for going out-of-network and had to pay most of the bill, if not all of it, out-of-pocket. The network would pay an in-network physician $62 but would penalize a patient for going to a physician that charged only $49 for the same service. And the uninsured patient that was paying his/her own bills always paid the inflated retail price. This does not make a lot of sense to me.

Then there are the hospital bills. I'll share one of hundreds to help make the point. A patient went to a network hospital for out-patient surgery and the total bill was $2,912. 81. The total amount paid by the insurance company and the individual was $838.00.

One position might be that the insurance company and the individual saved a lot of money by using the network—and they did. When you analyze it a little more, however, it becomes apparent that something is wrong here. First, if the patient's insurance plan had not been part of the network, he and/or his insurance company would have paid the full price of $2,912.81. If that individual had been paying for the service himself, the bill would have been $2,912.81. If that patient had been poor but determined to pay the bill (like the woman with the 1932 hospital bill described earlier) the price would have been $2,912.81.

Second, and even more disturbing, is the question about how the hospital arrived at $2,912.81 as the charge? If the amount paid ($838) actually covered the cost of providing the service along with a reasonable profit, why was there such an exorbitant mark up? If the $838 did not cover the cost, why did the hospital shift cost to the other insurance companies and private pay patients?

It is morally correct to discount services to those who do not have the ability to pay. It is not morally correct to discount healthcare services to those most able to pay at the expense of those with the least ability to pay. It is time to do away with network discounts and deal with price.

CHAPTER FIVE

FIXING THE FLAWS

A few years ago I met with the head of a major healthcare research project. When I said that healthcare delivery and finance in the United States is broken, he replied, "Healthcare in the U.S. IS NOT BROKEN, it is working exactly the way it was designed to work." Despite his outstanding credentials, I respectfully disagree. Healthcare delivery and finance in the U.S. was not designed—it evolved around financial systems and those systems are splintered and fractured. By definition they ARE BROKEN and it will take a consumer-led revolution to fix them.

Before you start fighting a war it is helpful to know who, or what, you are fighting. In other words, it helps to know your enemy. To fight with passion, and passion is a necessary component of winning a hard fight, it helps to know why you are fighting and what you are fighting for. So I will identify each opponent in our fight, why we are fighting them, and what we are fighting for. I'll present our opponents in alphabetical order since each fight is equally important and the alphabetical presentation makes it easier for me to explain why I "attacked" one first and another last. It is the closest thing to a bulletproof vest that I have at my disposal.

The first thing you need to understand about healthcare today is that IT IS ALL ABOUT MONEY AND POLITICS! It doesn't make any difference which element you are fighting to change—hospitals, insurance companies, pharmaceutical companies, physicians, laboratories, rehabilitation services, surgery centers, etc. IT IS ALL ABOUT MONEY AND POLITICS! And the lure of MONEY and POLITICAL influence is trumping your rights as a healthcare consumer.

The fact that healthcare IS ALL ABOUT MONEY has been the hardest thing for me to accept. When I began my healthcare career in 1965, healthcare was about mission, philosophy, and good patient care. Pay rates were low—my wife made significantly more in her first year of teaching in a Catholic school than I made as a registered medical (laboratory) technologist and I worked 12 months a year, weekends, holidays, and was on emergency night call every other night and every other weekend. Registered nurses made 25 cents an hour less than registered medical technologists. Most people in healthcare in those days (with the possible exception of some specialized physicians) could have applied the same amount of education toward another career and made a lot more money. In short, we were not there for the money. We were there because we liked the work and received a lot of personal satisfaction from doing our part to help those who were sick and injured. That may sound corny, but I believe it to be true. I'm sure that most in healthcare today still gain much personal satisfaction from caring for the sick and injured, but so much has changed in those 50+ years. We now need to examine the individual healthcare businesses more as opponents or adversaries than as allies.

HOSPITALS

It is honestly painful for me to include hospitals as an adversary because I think they should be our greatest allies. Unfortunately, they have fallen from the pedestal upon which they were held for more than a hundred years.

When I say hospitals are not our allies, I'm speaking of them as the institutions that have been sucked into the evolving healthcare financing system, and, in the process, lost focus of their original missions and philosophies and what should be their primary reason to exist—to improve the health status of the community they serve. I do not intend to demean in any way the hardworking, dedicated staff that labor under a myriad of rules, regulations, and constraints to care for those in need. I admit to being a part of the hospital institutional leadership that contributed to the mess we are in today. In retrospect, I'm not proud of some of the administrative decisions I supported, but hindsight is always 20/20.

I was raised under the philosophy that if you don't make a mistake once in a while, you are not doing much. That is not to say that you should try to make mistakes, but when you are traveling in un-chartered waters, mistakes will be made. Hospitals were in un-chartered waters from the time Medicare was implemented in 1968 through the medical technology boom of the 1970s and 1980s.

I was also raised under the philosophy that once you recognize that you have made a mistake, you own up to it and do everything possible to correct that mistake as soon as possible. That's where hospitals erred. Rather than work and fight collectively to right the ship, they slipped into a battle among themselves for money, power, and control, and they did it under the guise of competition.

Good, healthy competition is the vehicle that drives innovation and has allowed our country to prosper as no other. I am an advocate for competition and believe it will be a key factor in our fight to regain control of our healthcare. The error hospitals made was in the competitive model they chose.

The battlefield they chose was to compete through discounts to networks and insurance companies that forced people to use the hospital(s) that offered the biggest discount. Their competition was not, and still is not, based on price, quality, and customer service which are the market forces driving most businesses.

The original concept was for a network (often referred to as a Preferred Provider Organization or PPO) to have an exclusive agreement with a limited number of hospitals, thus forcing an increase in patient volume for those hospitals. Although the network discount model did not treat individuals like you and me very well, it did serve the financial interests of the hospitals. Over time, almost all hospitals, physicians, pharmacies and other healthcare service providers became part of a network – all give discounts to hold people captive in their network while those outside of the network pay full price. Full price is whatever the provider wants to charge and has little or nothing to do with the providers' actual costs.

Simply stated, the network discount model does not represent competition based on price, quality, and service. While serving as a hospital contract manager, I was involved in contract negotiations with networks for more than 15 years. I don't remember ever seeing "customer service" as a contract criterion and the only quality related item that needed to be satisfied was accreditation by the Joint Commission on the Accreditation of Healthcare Organizations. Very few hospitals couldn't maintain their accredited status.

I'll include more on the mistake of equating "charges" with "price." "Price" is the amount of money given and accepted for something of value. "Charges," at least in healthcare, are the starting point for discount negotiations. "High charge" hospitals and other healthcare service providers have an advantage over "low charge" service providers because the "high charge" provider can also be the "high discount" provider. Since networks focus on the size (percentage) of the discount, the "high charge" providers have an advantage when competing for network and insurance contracts. A hospital finance executive told me in August (2007) that at his hospital, the actual hospital cost is about 40% of what they charge.

My position on the competitive advantage of "high charge, high discount" providers was confirmed by an insurance consultant in Indianapolis, IN. I met with him to see if he would help market our consumer-driven program. After explaining how the program worked, he said, "Your approach is absolutely correct, but I cannot support it, because if I support that approach, I will put myself out of business. The only way I have to show my clients that I save them money is to show how much I saved them through discounts. Do away with discounts and you do away with my business." It appears that consultants are more interested in making money by selling artificial savings than in helping to create real savings through system reforms.

In Chapter Two I used my wife's 2007 rotator cuff surgery as an example of the hospital "discount game." To recap that example, in February of 2007, my wife had rotator cuff surgery at a local hospital. The total hospital "charges" were $22,205.81. The amount accepted by the hospital in payments from my insurance company and my co-payments (the "price") was $8,455.04. That is a discount of $13,750.77 or 61.9%.

Okay, that is an old example so let's update it a little. As I mentioned earlier, my grandson had an appendectomy in early April of this year (2019). The total charges were $53,986.53 with a discount (many call it a contractual allowance) of $10,726.06. That's roughly a 20% discount. It is now September, and my daughter is still trying to get itemized statements from both the hospital and insurance company.

Here's another one from some lab tests my wife just had at a local hospital earlier this year. Total charges - $134 and the discount was - $101.13. That's a 75% discount. Just one more and this one is from June 2019. I had some premalignant lesions destroyed on my arm and face. The total charge was $661 and the amount paid was $174.07 – a 74% discount. There is still pretty crazy stuff going on with "price" versus "charge."

So, what do we do about this? First, let's get our hospitals to stop trying to fill their beds and outpatient service departments with patients held hostage by networks, preferred provider organizations, and insurance contracts. The practice of giving discounts of 20% to 75% is borderline insanity. Offering a discount to everyone for prompt payment of bills is certainly reasonable, but let's go to a system where every purchaser of hospital services is charged the same and pays the same.

Hospitals need to publish their prices

Publishing prices, however, is not enough. Knowing the price of something without having quality indicators is almost worthless. Admittedly, hospital quality is extremely complex but that is no excuse for not providing it. The responsibility for making this complex information understandable to the ultimate consumer falls squarely on the shoulders of the hospitals.

Once you have price and quality information, you deserve some service guarantees. I remember my wife complaining that when she had an appointment for one of our children to see a pediatrician her typical wait time was two hours. Even when she would call to see if appointments were running on time she would be told, "Everything's on schedule." She would still have a two hour wait. Making the wait even worse was that she didn't just have the sick child to care for but she also had two other children with her to manage during the wait. More than 30 years ago, a now deceased physician in a nearby community had a sign in the reception area of his office and surgical clinic that said something to the effect of, "If we are more than 15 minutes late in seeing you at your appointed time, your charges will be reduced." Beside that sign was a discount schedule that started at 10%, but I don't remember where it went from there. Yes, some appointments and surgeries took longer than expected causing unavoidable delays for the patients that followed. This physician, however, recognized that those delays were not the fault of the waiting patients, and that the patients' time (and that of their families) was extremely valuable to them.

Hospital patients deserve no less. Medications should be administered correctly and on time, call lights and questions answered within a defined standard, and the value of peoples' time needs to be respected. *The bottom line—hospitals need to be competing based on price, quality and service—just like other businesses do in a free market system.*

INSURANCE COMPANIES

The purpose of an insurance company is to make money! There is nothing wrong with that. However, there should be a maximum profit from each insured person. Companies need to define their reserve pools and profit based on the number of people they insure. Profits in excess of that pre-defined amount should be returned to those paying the premium. This could be done in the form of credits toward future premiums or as a credit to the individuals' Health Savings Accounts. Under this approach, an insurance company increases its profits by creating programs that attract more business. In short, they make more money by serving more people.

Instead of working with networks to obtain artificial savings through discounts from inflated charges, insurance companies are in an ideal position to work with healthcare service providers to develop "best practice" care packages for individuals with diabetes, heart disease, various cancers, etc. Insurance companies have all of the information—start using it constructively for the benefit of all.

Insurance companies can offer some creative programs that help individuals understand the benefit of living healthy lifestyles. If people choose to smoke, to be obese, or not keep their blood pressure, cholesterol, etc. under control, that is their choice—but you should not be forced to pay for their excesses!

How about a plan that has its premiums set assuming that everyone in the plan pool is morbidly obese, smokes, has high blood pressure, has elevated cholesterol, etc? Then each person in the pool receives a premium credit for each lifestyle factor they keep within normal ranges. Individuals increase or lose premium credits based on annual health screening evaluations.

If an individual chooses not to participate in a health screening, that is their choice. If someone chooses to continue smoking, that is their choice. If someone chooses to remain overweight, that is their choice. However, this plan does reduce the financial burden of those choosing to live healthy lifestyles. You may not have the right to tell someone how much they should weigh, but neither do they have the right to pass on the costs of their excesses to you!

Health Savings Accounts (HSAs) give individuals the opportunity to accumulate savings for future medical costs during their younger years when their consumption of healthcare resources is low. When coupled with very low cost basic care, these savings allow individuals to purchase high deductible plans to provide an incentive to care about cost and utilization, insure against catastrophic loss and, over time, can provide the funding for supplemental Medicare coverage and some or all of the cost for nursing home insurance. Insurance companies need to offer many options for incorporating HSAs into their insurance products.

Insurance companies are in the ideal position to identify the relatively small percentage of physicians that abuse the system. Once these individuals are identified, the insurance companies should impose all of the rules and regulations necessary to control them, but the insurers should allow the other physicians (the largest majority) to practice medicine without having to ask, "Mother, May I?" We'll address this more later.

The technology is available today to allow insurance companies to do real-time processing of most claims. Banks have been moving money electronically between individuals, merchants, and other banks for decades. That technology should be applied to settling all but the most complicated medical claims.

Insurance companies can be a true system-wide value added entity by developing programs that help "right" some of the "wrongs" they helped to create.

NETWORKS

Networks restrict choice, add overhead costs, drive healthcare provider charges up, and oftentimes are the cause for individuals to change from using their preferred physician or hospital to using ones they don't like, are less convenient, are farther away, or possibly are even of lesser quality. Either get rid of networks or force them to develop some value added services. Networks could work with insurance companies and healthcare service providers to develop the "best practice" care packages for individuals with specific medical conditions. Networks could be the backbone for the sharing of what various healthcare service providers charge for their services. This could be linked with quality and service information. There are a number of things the established networks could do to help "right" the "wrongs" that they, at least in part, brought to the system.

Whatever they do, networks must help end the high charge, big discount environment they helped to create!

PHYSICIANS

As with hospitals, physicians need to stop trying to fill their appointment calendars with patients held hostage by network, preferred provider organizations, and insurance contracts. Physicians giving networks, preferred provider organizations, and insurance companies large discounts at the same time they demand full charges form individuals paying cash is just plain wrong! A recently retired family practice physician did have a sign in his office stating that uninsured patients paying at the time of service would receive the same discount he extended to insurance companies. I gave him kudos for taking action to correct the gross inequity.

Let's end the discounts and get to a system where every purchaser of physician services is charged the same and pays the same! Like hospitals, physicians need to publish their prices.

As with hospitals, publishing prices is not enough. Knowing the price of something without having quality indicators is almost worthless. As stated before, healthcare quality information is extremely complex but that is no excuse for not providing it. The responsibility of making this complex information understandable to the ultimate consumer falls squarely on the shoulders of the physicians.

Once you have price and quality information, you deserve some service guarantees. Think about the physician I told you about that had a sign in the reception area of his office and surgical clinic that said something to the effect of, "If we are more than 15 minutes late in seeing you at your appointed time, your charges will be reduced." You deserve no less from your physician—his/her time may be very valuable, but so is yours!

The bottom line—physicians need to compete based on price, quality and service just like most businesses do in a free market system.

POLITICIANS (GOVERNMENT)

Healthcare is a political "hot potato" but you can influence your elected officials to do what is necessary and right. The first thing to talk to politicians about is the need for them to work for the right, long-term solutions to the healthcare business problems—not the short-term, political solutions that promise quick, painless solutions that give everyone gold plated healthcare at someone else's expense. If a politician promises a quick and/or inexpensive solution, don't let him/her get away with making the promise without providing you with all of the nitty-gritty details. Remember the promises of the Affordable Care Act – You can keep your doctor; You can keep your hospital; You can keep your insurance plan; Everyone will have insurance. Term limits may be the best solution to keeping politicians from making promises they neither can keep nor intend to keep after getting your vote.

Help your elected officials understand that what we need most from the government(s) is sound policy that creates a level playing field for all healthcare service providers and drives the healthcare business toward the free market model. They also have a role in creating a nationwide insurance pool for catastrophic medical expenses, creating nationwide competition among insurance companies, and supporting programs for the financially indigent. They also need to focus as much on access to care as they do on the numbers of people that are insured or uninsured. Remember, insurance coverage does not mean access.

Possibly the best role for government would be to help solve the physician shortage problem. It is projected that physician demand will grow faster than the supply and that there will be a shortfall of between 42,600 and 123,300 physicians by 2030. The projected shortage of primary care physicians is between 14,800 and 49,300 and for non-primary care physicians the projection is 33,800 to 72,700 by 2030.[55] The government helped to create the shortage with the Balanced Budget Act of 1997 which set a broad limit on training positions according to what Medicare would fund. It's time for our politicians to participate in solving the problem. First, they can help make primary care a much more attractive career option for medical students. Second, they can help to drastically expand the number of internal medicine and family medicine residency slots. Third, they can help to reduce the bureaucracy involved in the practice of primary care.[56] I'll add a fourth, expand the capacities of medical schools. The state of Indiana has an excellent program that couples the Indiana University School of Medicine with several universities in the state including Purdue, Notre Dame, and Ball State. It has proven to be an efficient way to expand medical school capacity without developing another school of medicine.

When you hear a politician talk about implementing an insurance program run by the federal government, ask them this: "Why should I trust my healthcare, and that of my loved ones, to the same

---

[55] HIS Markit Ltd: The Complexities of Physician Supply and Demand: Projections from 2016 to 2030, March 2018

[56] Dhand, Suneel, MD: Solving the physician shortage requires these 3 things to happen, MEDPAGE Today, February 16, 2015

government that runs the inefficient Veterans Administration system, Medicare, Medicaid, and Social Security—all of which have broken promises, are under-funded and headed toward financial disaster?"

Healthcare is replete with moral, ethical, religious and emotional issues that are next to impossible to solve on a national basis. These issues are best left to the states to resolve within their citizen voters. Individual medical needs are not an unalienable right the government has to guarantee.

CHAPTER SIX

BEFORE WE CAN FIX IT

Before we delve into the specific proposals to improve our healthcare programs, there are a few things we have to understand about healthcare as a business and consensus must be reached on the responsibilities of individuals, insurance companies, state government and federal government. This will not be easy, but for solutions to be put forward, they must be defined. For the purpose of my proposals, I will define them in ways that, at least to me, seem fair and reasonable. I do so with the understanding that many, if not most people, will disagree vehemently with some or all of them.

THE HEALTHCARE BUSINESS

You work to make money. The business you work for has to make money for the owners or shareholders. Even a not-for-profit social service business or agency without profit motives needs revenue in excess of expenses or they will go out of business. It all boils down to the bottom line!

The healthcare business isn't any different. Physicians practice medicine to make a living—a socially acceptable term for profit. Insurance companies exist for the sole purpose of making money. For-profit hospitals are in business to make money. The not-for-profit hospitals' income that exceeds expenses may not go to the benefit of shareholders, but let's call the excess revenue what it is—profit! Pharmaceutical manufacturers are in business to make a profit. Ambulatory surgery centers and urgent care centers are in business to make money.

Then there are all of those other ancillary healthcare services like physical therapy centers, oxygen and respiratory service providers, physician & hospital networks, equipment and supply vendors, etc. They are all in business to make money! Many in the not-for-profit sector will take issue with that statement but they will also admit that if there is no margin, there is no mission. Unfortunately, it is my observation that many of the not-for-profit healthcare businesses, especially general, acute care hospitals, now focus more on the bottom line and market share than they do on mission.

It's that simple—all businesses need a positive bottom line or they will eventually go out of business.

I assume that you are an honest person, that you are proud of the product(s) and service (s) you provide, and that you want those you serve to be satisfied so you will get repeat and referred business. I also assume you are a good employee who works hard and your employer tries to provide you with a good work environment. All of that applies equally to healthcare employees and businesses.

It is probably also safe to assume that the business you work in is constantly changing and has to keep pace with technology and the changing business environment or it will go out of business. So it is for healthcare businesses.

The business you work in probably has a lot of regulatory agencies looking over its shoulder, as do those in healthcare businesses.

We could march down this path for several more pages but you get the picture—the things that make the business you work for and healthcare businesses similar far outnumber the things that make them different. At least, that is, from the business perspective.

So, if healthcare businesses and your business have so much in common, why are healthcare costs out of control and your costs are not? It really isn't that complicated.

There are seven primary factors that separate healthcare businesses from most other businesses. Those factors are:

1. In healthcare, someone else pays most of the bill, i.e., insurance company or government.
2. In healthcare, true consumer competition does not exist.
3. In healthcare, administrative costs are excessive.
4. Healthcare flourishes on the cost-shift, that is, charging the paying patient more to make up the loss from serving patients that cannot pay.
5. There are excessive costs associated with defensive medicine, i.e., ordering tests for the primary purpose of avoiding lawsuits.
6. In healthcare, new technology is mostly additive. For example, you could have a CAT scan, followed by an MRI, followed by a PET scan. One does not replace the other, it adds to it.
7. Healthcare is influenced by more moral and ethical issues.

INSURANCE

The concept of insurance extends back to ancient times when people hunted in groups to reduce the risk of injury from animal attacks. In Babylonia, King Hammurabi established the "Hammurabi Code" that forgave a person's debt in case of a personal catastrophe like property loss or death. Ancient farmers transporting their crops on reed boats would place their crops on multiple boats so that if a few boats sank, they would only lose a portion of their crop.

In the 1600's ships transporting goods to and from America were sometimes lost at sea. Ship owners began posting their cargo and destinations in London coffeehouses and rich merchants would sign under the posting (thus the term underwriting) agreeing to fund the trip in exchange for a percentage of the trips profit. If the ship sank, the ship owner's loss was protected. This was the origin of Lloyds of London that also developed fire insurance following the great London fire in 1666.

The point is that the original purpose of insurance was to protect against catastrophic loss. Even the first healthcare plan in America was a prepaid hospital plan. In 1929, teachers at Baylor University in Dallas, Texas signed an agreement with the nearby hospital that they would pay an incremental stipend in return for full hospital care – insurance against the catastrophic loss that could occur from a long hospital stay.

Today, healthcare insurance is more than insuring against catastrophic loss – people want it to cover everything related to healthcare. Therein lies a major problem. When you buy automobile insurance you don't expect the insurance company to pay for your routine maintenance expenses like oil changes, new tires, new brakes, air filters, etc. Car insurance is to protect you against the catastrophic loss associated with an accident, vandalism, etc. You plan for and budget for the routine maintenance of your car and save money to cover the deductible associated with your insurance plan. Same goes for homeowners insurance. You buy protection against a catastrophic loss but save to cover routine maintenance and deductibles. This leads us to the next section.

INDIVIDUAL RESPONSIBILITY

In chapter two I wrote a section on individual responsibility. There are two elements of that section I believe must be repeated here. The first is that for the most part, individuals have been sheltered from the true cost of healthcare. Their employer pays most of the insurance premium; the individual has low deductibles, low co-payments, and low coinsurance. As a result, the perception is that healthcare is free, or at least almost free. The individual has little reason to care about how much healthcare services cost or how many of them are consumed. A short time ago (July 11, 2019 to be exact) I overheard two women talking and one was telling the other about an outpatient surgery statement she had just received for around $43,000. She was chuckling about it and said, "That's such a crazy amount but it doesn't matter. I have to pay $1,000 and insurance takes care of the rest."

The other statement that is important to repeat is the quote from Dennis Prager – "Most people do not yearn to be free. Most people yearn to be taken care of." I don't want you to infer from this that I believe people are basically lazy or don't care even though some may be. My wife was a substitute teacher for a few years and told me about a third grade boy she was helping with some arithmetic and he didn't seem to care. She told him he would need to know arithmetic when he got older and had a job. She asked him what he wanted to do when he grew up and she was startled when he said, "Nothing!" She then asked how he would earn the money to have a place to live, buy food and cloths, etc. She was equally startled when he responded with, "I'll just do welfare. My mom does welfare. My grandma does welfare. I'll just do that."

I have to admit that my first reaction to this story was that the boy is just lazy or at least being raised to be lazy. After pondering it over the years I think that reaction was wrong. Yes, there may be some lazy people but I think they comprise a very small percentage of our population. I don't think that either the little boy or his mother or grandmother were necessarily lazy – they just did not have the incentives to do any better. The government was taking care of them.

It's like the lady in the parking lot I mentioned above. She recognized how "crazy" the amount of the bill was but she was not incentivized to care or to be part of changing things. Most people do respond to incentives and one of the strongest incentives for most is money. Spending other peoples' money is pretty easy but people tend to be a little more cautious when spending their own.

Change has never been easy or fast and it won't be when it comes to changing attitudes about healthcare. Fifty years ago about 42 percent of adults in the United States smoked. It was acceptable pretty much everywhere – offices, hospitals, restaurants, etc. Following decades of education and awareness programs coupled with the banning of smoking in public places the percent of smokers has been reduced to 13.9 percent.[57]

Since healthcare costs affect virtually everyone, I believe that with a strong effort by governments, businesses and individuals we can make significant changes within five to ten years. To do so will require that people begin to experience the real cost of healthcare and fully recognize that nothing is free. Healthcare insurance paid by an employer is not free – it is paid for by those buying the products or services provided by the employer. Healthcare coverage paid by the government (Medicare, Medicaid, etc.) is not free – it is paid for by taxing working individuals and businesses. Healthcare provided at no charge through clinics and hospitals is not free – it is paid for with tax dollars or by shifting the cost to paying patients.

The bottom line, if we are to gain control of healthcare costs is that individuals must be incentivized to care and to get involved. Once that happens, change can come rather quickly. Just look at what has happened with the costs of Lasik surgery. Since 1995 the charge for Lasik surgery has trended downward. It is a highly competitive business that is not covered by insurance so people shop for price and quality. Retail prices generally range from $1,000-$3,000 per eye but it is quite common for providers to have "specials" at reduced prices and many offer long-term financing options. I've even seen ads for as low as $220 per eye but those prices wouldn't apply to very many people. We need to put the same principle to work for the majority of healthcare. That means individuals must have a significant amount of their money involved in healthcare purchasing decisions. I'm not speaking about emergency situations like an accident, heart attack or stroke. I'm speaking about all of the things an individual can get involved in like shopping for prescription drug prices, laboratory test

[57] Searing, Linda: The Big Number: Number of U.S. adult smokers hits all-time low, The Washington Post, June 23, 2018

prices, CT and MRI scan prices, hospital and physician prices that are not life threatening emergencies like joint replacements.

GOVERNMENT

I'm going to reflect for a moment on the civics lessons I received during my K-12 days several decades ago. I know this isn't necessary for most that will be reading this book but in the event there are a few younger readers I feel compelled to quell my fear that their civics education was less than adequate. Even though presented in an extremely simplified manner, I'll feel better for having including it.

The purpose of our Federal Government, as found in the Preamble of the Constitution, is to "establish Justice, insure domestic Tranquility, provide for the Common Defense, promote the General Welfare, and secure the Blessings of Liberty to ourselves and our posterity.

State Governments have the duty to administer roads, education, public safety, justice and other as determined by voters, state lawmakers, and the constitution of the state. States take on all of the powers not specifically granted to the U.S. Federal government, according to the 10th Amendment to the United States Constitution.

Local government provides goods and services and involves citizens in determining specific local public needs and how those needs can be met. Even though the federal government has the power to compel states to take certain actions, it is the farthest from the people and the least capable of making laws and regulations that represent all of the people. The federal government, state and local governments must work together and we must guard against the federal government usurping authorities that should be left to the state and local governments that are closest to the citizens they serve.

We elect politicians that may have entered the political arena pure of heart but it seems a majority quickly come under the strong influence of the funding provided by special interest groups. Their path to re-election is to bend to the wishes of the best funded special interests and pay less attention to what the majority of the citizens they represent may actually want or need. Often times re-election depends upon "giving" something to people disguised as "free" or under some other false pretense. I remember the federal funding for "shovel-ready" construction projects. I was involved in seeking some of those funds for a building project and although it was not really "shovel-ready" we received the funding. The funding was also accompanied by a federal bureaucracy to manage the funds and assure they were spent according to the rules. The point is that about everything the federal government does is accompanied by an expansion of the bureaucracy. The problem is that those staffing the bureaucracy are not elected and they are not accountable to anyone and once established the bureaucracy never goes away and continues to be more intrusive and controlling of businesses and individuals.

It's obvious I am not a fan of big, out of control, intrusive government. That said, the federal government does have an important and necessary role in solving the healthcare cost issues and we'll address that in some detail later. It will just be incumbent upon all of us to keep it in its place and we do that be keeping a keen eye on our senators and representatives. If they don't represent what you want, vote against them in the next election and financially support an opponent that represents your values.

BUSINESS AND EMPLOYEES

I think this is the time to mention something that is seldom, if ever, included in healthcare cost discussions and that is the part business has played in creating some of the issues associated with the problems we have today. As noted in the introduction, during World War II employers used healthcare benefits as a means to attract skilled labor. A price/wage freeze was in effect and businesses were successful in obtaining a ruling that healthcare benefits could be provided as a non-wage, tax-exempt employee benefit. Following the war, labor began including healthcare benefits in contract negotiations and, because healthcare insurance was inexpensive and welcomed by all, the businesses acceded to the demands. Within a few years, healthcare benefits became part of the compensation package of most large businesses and industries and smaller businesses had to follow suit to attract needed employees.

For several decades organized labor accomplished many great things for our country. Their work lead to the Fair Labor Standards Act of 1938 that established the 40 hour work week, the minimum wage (25 cents per hour then), overtime pay and a prohibition of child labor. They were also instrumental in the passage of the Occupational Safety & Health Act of 1970 covering safety in the workplace. Coal miners, textile workers and millions of others have benefited greatly from these actions.

Despite the great accomplishments, I believe labor has also had a deleterious effect in many cases. One of my biggest concerns is that labor unions create division – division between union and nonunion workers, between workers and employers, and disrupt the relationship between the job and economics. I become infuriated when I read of employers being sued over things like paid time to change clothes. In my mind this falls into the category of negotiating for more money for less work and I include negotiating for more healthcare benefits in this category.

By labor demanding, and business succumbing to the demands, an expectation of gold-plated, Cadillac medicine for everyone at someone else's expense is created. It makes no difference if the "someone else's money" is from the business or the government it is still someone else's money! A business gets its money from customers buying a service or product – that is someone else's money! The government gets its money from taxes – it isn't government's money, it is someone else's money!

If we are to gain any control over healthcare consumption and pricing the purchase of healthcare services must include some of each individual's money and it has to be more than a small copay. That will sound harsh to many, but unless people are spending some of their own money, they will never be incentivized to care about cost. It is all about money and some of that money has to come out of the individual's pocket! It is that simple! How to get there while providing necessary care to all is the hard part. That's what we will tackle in Chapter Seven.

LET'S BRING IT ALL TOGETHER AND FIX IT!

Let's begin by reviewing a few facts about healthcare in the United States.

1. 91.2 percent of our population had health insurance coverage for all or part of 2017.
2. 67.2 percent had private health insurance with the majority (56.0 percent) having employer-based insurance with Medicaid, Medicare, and military programs covering the balance.[58]
3. About half of those that are uninsured are eligible for coverage under an existing program.
4. Health insurance coverage does not mean access to healthcare.
5. People with health insurance have increasingly higher deductibles they are responsible for paying.

---

[58] Berchick, Edward R., Hood, Emily, and Barnett, Jessica C., Health Insurance Coverage in the United States, United States Census Bureau, September 12, 2018

6. The provider (hospital, doctor, pharmacy, etc.) charges have nothing to do with the price actually paid by the insurance company.
7. Medicare is inadequately funded for an aging population with longer life expectancies.
8. Making substantive improvements to our health insurance programs will take several years and will necessitate all parties cooperating and focusing on what is best for the country as a whole – not special interests.

THE UNINSURED

Since 8.8 percent of the population is uninsured, and about half of those are eligible for existing programs, let's focus on that group first. In reality, that may be the easiest of the problems we have to fix. We learn from United States Census Bureau data[59] for 2017 that most of the uninsured were working-age adults. Most (84.6 percent) were 19 to 64 year-olds. 1 in 4 were 26-34 years old and about 1 in 5 people ages 34-44. About 4 in 10 of the uninsured were non-Hispanic white and the uninsured were disproportionately concentrated in the South. Approximately 50% of the uninsured in 2017 were in the South followed by the West (about 21%), the Midwest (about 17%) and the Northeast (about 12%) – these percentages are my estimates from graphs shown in the publication.

Even following passage of the Affordable Care Act, 45 percent of uninsured adults said they remained uninsured because the cost of coverage was too high and in 2017 one in five went without needed medical care due to cost.[60] Medicaid coverage has been expanded to nearly all adults with incomes below 138 percent of poverty. Subsidies are available for those above 138 percent of poverty but some still

[59] Berchick, Edward, Most Uninsured Were Working-Age Adults, United States Census Bureau, September 12, 2018
[60] Facts about the Uninsured Population, Kaiser Family Foundation, December 7, 2018

believe it is too expensive. The Children's Health Insurance Program (CHIP) provides comprehensive benefits to children and my focus here will be limited to uninsured adults.

There is also an issue with those who don't know that they can get help and this may largely be due to lack of education. In the city of Baltimore in 2017 there were 13 high schools and one middle school with zero students proficient in reading and math. I'm not picking on Baltimore but those numbers were reported on a couple of news programs just before I started this section. I'm certain that a majority of schools, especially those in large cities, have some students that just can't make it academically. But it appears the problem may not be isolated to inner city schools in depressed cities. The Nation's Report Card data from 2017 shows the following percentages of students at or above proficient for grade 12: Civics – 12%; Economics – 42%; Geography – 20%; Mathematics – 25%; Reading – 37%; Science – 22%; U.S. History – 12%; and Writing – 27%. There can be many causes for this including that our educational system is nearing total collapse but it is not within the scope of this writing to delve into the subject. However, if a person cannot read, write, or do simple math, they most likely will be relegated to low paying jobs and if their employer does not offer health insurance benefits, they will be covered by Medicaid. However, they do have to apply and it is the responsibility of cities and towns to make resources available to help them do so.

An estimated 25 percent of the uninsured are non-citizens. These include both lawfully present and undocumented immigrants.[61] Undocumented immigrants are ineligible for federally funded health coverage, but legal immigrants can qualify for subsidies in the Marketplaces and those who have been in the country for more than five years are eligible for Medicaid.[62]

---

[61] Kaiser Family Foundation analysis of 2017 American Community Survey, 1-Year Estimates

[62] Health Coverage of Immigrants (Washington, DC: Kaiser Family Foundation, December 2017)

Before we get to what we are going to do about the uninsured, there are two basic questions we need to answer. 1) Where does healthcare fall between the two extremes - a privilege or a right. A privilege in which the only healthcare a person gets is that for which they can pay and a right in which everyone gets all of the healthcare they need or want regardless of whether or not they can pay. 2) Who pays as we move on that line extending between a privilege and a right?

Picture a line starting on the left with "A Privilege" at zero on a ten point scale and going to the right with "A Right" being at ten on the scale. I think that most would agree that some healthcare is at minimum a "necessity" that falls somewhere to the right of privilege. However, as it approaches the right of the scale it becomes necessary to define how much healthcare is "a right" versus "a necessity" or "a privilege." A perfect compromise would put healthcare at five on the scale with some healthcare "a right" that everyone is entitled to and some "a privilege" that people get if they can pay for it. You can probably ask 100 people where on the scale healthcare should fall and you will likely get 100 different responses. We are an extremely diverse country and that's what makes this so difficult. My goal is to make recommendations that a majority of common, everyday citizens will find to be reasonable while understanding that those leaning toward one or other of the extremes will not be happy.

Medicaid is a program administered by the states and funded by both federal and state monies. In 2017 the average percent of the Medicaid money provided by the federal government was 61.5 percent and the states averaged paying 38.5 percent. There is significant funding variation between states with one having 80 percent paid by the federal government and another receiving less than 50 percent.

The following are Mandatory Medicaid Benefits:

Inpatient hospital services	Outpatient hospital services	Nursing facility services
Home health services	Physician services	Rural health clinic services
Laboratory and X-ray services	Family planning services	Nurse midwife services
Federally qualified health center services	Transportation to medical care	Tobacco cessation counseling for pregnant women
EPSDT: Early and Periodic EPSDT: Early and Periodic Screening, Diagnostic, and Treatment services	Certified Pediatric and Family Certified Pediatric and Family Nurse Practitioner services	Freestanding Birth Center Freestanding Birth Center services (when licensed or otherwise recognized by the state)

The following are optional benefits that states may cover if they choose:

Prescription Drugs	Clinic services	Physical Therapy
Occupational therapy	Respiratory care services	Podiatry services
Optometry services	Dental services	Dentures
Prosthetics	Eyeglasses	Chiropractic services
Other practitioner services	Private duty nursing services	Personal Care
Hospice	Case management	TB related services

Other diagnostic, screening, preventive and rehabilitative services	Speech, hearing and language disorder services	Community First Choices Option- 1915(k)
Self-Directed Personal Assistance Services- 1915(j)	Inpatient psychiatric services for individuals under age 21	Other services approved by the Secretary
Services for Individuals Age 65 or Older in an Institution for Mental Disease ((IMD)	State Plan Home and Community Based Services- 1915(i)	Health Homes for Enrollees with Chronic Conditions – Section 1945
Services in an intermediate care facility for individuals with Intellectual Disability		

The Mandatory Medicaid Benefits appears to be a reasonable definition of the basic healthcare benefits our country has agreed upon that should be guaranteed to all of our citizens. It would not be unreasonable to increase the eligibility from 138 percent of poverty to 150 percent of poverty to cover another segment of the uninsured. Any expansion of the benefits must be enacted and paid for by the states and such expansions must be approved by a vote of legal voting citizens. Citizens of this country should not be required to participate in the payment for any services not included in the Mandatory Medicaid Benefits unless specifically voted on by the state's citizens. Yes, this includes services such as gender reassignment services and surgeries, uterus transplants and the myriad of similar services yet unknown. We are a country of limited resources and as harsh as it may be, some things must remain "a privilege."

For the uninsured above 150 percent of poverty each state should offer a private plan to resident citizens of the state that mirrors the Mandatory Medicaid Benefits. This plan should be provided on a sliding fee scale between 150 percent of poverty and 200 percent of poverty.

Those people not qualifying for Medicaid and choosing not to participate in a state's sliding fee scale Medicaid mirror plan will have to seek care at their expense from urgent care centers, community health clinics and in the case of true emergencies, hospital emergency departments. As a society we must recognize that people have an individual responsibility to participate in programs available to them or suffer the consequences.

As of this writing the United States is a country of laws. We should not reward those who break our laws. We are a country that welcomes immigrants that come here legally. We have a moral and ethical obligation to have a way to provide the basic life sustaining healthcare to those who enter our country illegally but nothing more. These individuals will be cared for through community health clinics, urgent care centers and when necessary through hospital emergency departments. Charges for services rendered that the individual cannot pay will be the responsibility first of the city, then the county and finally the state. The residents and companies of these government jurisdictions can decide by vote how many illegal residents they choose to support. Federal enforcement agencies are available, ready and willing to help with the removal of people in our country illegally. Unfortunately, our elected officials in Washington are more responsive to special interest groups than to what individuals and states want and need. They also appear to think money grows on trees and that they will never run out of other people's money to spend. We need to either enforce the current immigration laws or change them and the states and their citizens need to be involved in making those changes. Since our legislators are reluctant to take illegal immigration seriously, we need to keep the costs for supporting the illegals as close to the local level as possible.

HEALTH SAVINGS ACCOUNTS

Health Savings Accounts (HSA) allow individuals to accumulate money to meet higher deductibles, co-payments, plus other out of pocket medical expenses and save for the future. To create a consumer-driven healthcare finance and delivery system, it is necessary for individuals to be spending some of their own money. However, the average individual today does not have the ability to meet $5,000 to $10,000 deductibles without some help. Every health insurance plan should include an HSA!

Transitioning to high deductibles, a necessary step to return insurance to its original purpose—insuring against the catastrophic loss, needs to be done over time and will pay the biggest dividends for those entering the system under age 45. The phase-in could be done over a five year period allowing individuals to build their HSAs as deductible increases. Many employees already use Section 125 plans that allow employees to use pre-tax dollars to pay for anticipated medical and certain other expenses. The problem with Section 125 is that if the individual miscalculates and has too much deducted from their pay, they lose it. Any medical expense dollars set aside under Section 125 should be moved to an HSA where the money rolls over from year to year. Additionally, as employers move to higher deductible plans, they will need to direct some of their premium savings into the employees' HSAs. This may be a hard pill to swallow, but it is essential to help individuals generate the funds in their HSAs needed to meet the higher deductibles. Individuals building their HSAs through retirement will have money to help pay insurance premiums if they retire before becoming eligible for Medicare or have money to help pay for a good Medicare supplement insurance plan as well as the Medicare drug donut hole.

Here is an example of how this worked out for a couple that asked me to analyze insurance plans in 2017. The couple was in their mid-forties with two small children. The husband, who obtained the family's health insurance through his employer, was changing employers for a higher paying job and needed to select which of the new plans he would enroll in. I'll cover the basics but keep the explanation as simple as possible. The plan he was leaving (I'll refer to it as the Old Traditional Plan (OTP)) was a very good plan with a deductible of $1,500, a maximum Out of Pocket of $4,500 and an annual premium for the employee of $13,200 for the family plan.

His choices of plans was 1) a New Traditional Plan (NTP) with a deductible of $4,000, a maximum Out of Pocket of $8,000 and an annual premium for the employee of $11,121 for the family plan and 2) a Health Savings Account (HSA) plan with a deductible of $12,700, a maximum Out of Pocket of $12,700, and an annual premium for the employee of $7,229 for the family plan. All of the plans provided preventive care at no charge and the employer made a $1,000 annual contribution to the HSA plan.

At first glance you might think that even with a higher maximum exposure of $3,500 the lower annual premium of $2,079 makes choosing the NTP a no-brainer - but not so fast. This is where it gets a little more complicated. The OTP had a maximum Out of Pocket exposure of $4,500 and the HSA plan has a maximum Out of Pocket exposure of $12,700 so the difference in maximum exposure between the OTP and the HSA plan is $8,200. The annual premium for the HSA plan is $5,971 less than the OTP premium. Going with the HSA plan and putting the $5,971 savings in premiums into the HSA and then adding the $1,000 employer HSA contribution the HSA plan maximum exposure is $5,729 versus $4,500 for the OTP. Oddly enough, applying the same analysis to the NTP the maximum exposure for it ($5,921) is actually higher than the HSA plan.

I explained the financial risk of choosing the HSA plan if they were unlucky and had a catastrophic medical expense during the first year before they had built a significant HSA. The couple decided they could take that risk and chose to go with the HSA plan and put the

$5,971 premium difference in their HSA. They have not experienced any catastrophic medical expenses in the last two years and now have a healthy HSA.

Let's assume they continue this program for 20 years when they will reach age 65 and have a similar healthcare expense experience similar to that of my wife and me. None of our four children had any major medical expenses while under our insurance plans; my wife had a major surgery and our prescription medications were negligible until after we reached age 65 (even now we'd be paying less than $1,000 per year if we were paying retail pharmacy prices). With these assumptions they would have an HSA in excess of $125,000 at age 65. If a portion of the HSA is invested in mutual funds or other safe investment just imagine what that number could be!

ESTABLISHING PROVIDER QUALITY INFORMATION

Asking people to shop for healthcare without giving them some information to help them make fully informed decisions is asking them to only consider cost. People need to have some quality information to make sound value judgments. This one is a challenge to say the least. First of all, quality in healthcare is difficult to define. In healthcare, it is not uncommon to have everything done absolutely right and still have an unfavorable result, even death. It is also possible to do almost everything wrong and have a favorable result. Then, there is everything between these two extremes.

I think of photography as 1/3 art, 1/3 science, and 1/3 luck. I can control the art and the science but I cannot control the luck. I don't know that medicine is 1/3 art, 1/3 science, and 1/3 luck, but I do believe that all three elements are present in the practice of medicine. There is unquestionably more emphasis on art and science, but a little luck also comes into play at times.

It is essential for people to understand that medicine, like weather forecasting, is not a perfect science. Several conditions can have similar signs and symptoms. People also describe their symptoms and health history differently. One person may be extremely detailed in what they tell their physician while another may skim the surface and omit information that could be essential for a quick, accurate diagnosis. The threshold of pain among people is very different. A person with a low threshold of pain may describe pain as excruciating while someone with an extremely high threshold might describe the same pain as mild. Some people go to their physician almost every time they sneeze while others wait until they are almost on their deathbed before they go to their physician. One patient responds quite well to a medication and someone else does not. The point is, everyone is different, every case is different, and you can't be 100% sure of what you are dealing with until all of the pieces of the puzzle are in place.

I think it is somewhat like putting a jigsaw puzzle together. The puzzle can include a picture of what appears in all respects to be a horse. However, until you find the piece(s) that contain the forehead of the animal, you don't know for sure if you have a horse or a unicorn.

Another problem in medicine is that it is not uncommon for a physician to have to make a decision without having all of the pieces of the puzzle. The physician may be at a point when a treatment decision has to be made and he may be forced to look at the puzzle and make a decision with some of the pieces missing. He might have to think through it like this. It has the feet of a horse. It has the tail of a horse. It has the body of a horse. It has the nose, ears, and mane of a horse. I know it could be a unicorn, but there are millions of horses and I don't know of anyone who has reported actually seeing a unicorn. Therefore, I'm going to treat it like a horse. If a day or two later, the final piece of the puzzle falls into place and the physician learns he had a unicorn rather than a horse, does that mean the physician practiced poor quality medicine? No! He was just unlucky. The piece of the puzzle that showed the unicorn's horn had not fallen into place before the decision had to be made. Medicine is like life — when you reach a decision point, you have to make the best decision you can with the information you have available to you at the time. Only hindsight is always 20/20!

If we can agree that medicine is not a perfect science, and that whatever we use to measure the quality of medicine will not be perfect, then we can start to examine some indicators that can be useful in assessing quality in healthcare. While I'm not an expert in assessing the quality of healthcare services, I do feel comfortable in stating that there are differences in quality between physicians, hospitals, and other healthcare providers. I also know that a lot of quality related information is collected and that very little of it is available to consumers.

Although assessing quality in healthcare is difficult, many organizations have been working on programs and systems to support quality-based decisions in healthcare. One such organization is Leapfrog that publishes a Hospital Safety Score. There are more than 2,000 hospitals participating in the voluntary program and they are assigned a grade from A to F representing the facility's ability to prevent injuries, errors, and infections. I went to www.leapfroggroup. org/compare and looked at the reports on the 13 acute care hospitals within 50 miles of my home. I was disappointed to see that only two are participating in the 2019 survey. There are about 5,200 acute care hospitals in the United States and I have to wonder what the 3,000 or so that don't participate have to hide. Leapfrog also has some very interesting specialized reports like the one on High-Risk Surgeries Performed at American Hospitals. Their data shows the minimum number of the procedures that should be performed at a hospital and the minimum number that a surgeon should perform each year to maintain proficiency. The report shows that for Bariatric Surgery for Weight Loss only 38 percent of reporting hospitals meet or exceed Leapfrogs minimum standards. All of this is available to businesses and individuals at no charge.

There are other sites like www.medicare.gov/hospitalcompare/ compare.html that also provides hospital quality information but Medicare and Leapfrog ask different questions and the grades will not mirror each other. www.Healthgrades.com is another site for comparing quality among hospitals and the basic information is free. For a small fee, detailed information can be obtained on hospitals and physicians. Surf around and you can learn about the National Committee for Quality Assurance (NCQA), the Health Plan Employer Data and Information Set (HEDIS), the American Medical Association (AMA), the Joint Commission on Accreditation of Healthcare Organizations (JACHO), and many others. As deductibles and copayments increase for individuals their demand for cost and quality information will intensify so healthcare providers that don't jump on the transparency train will be left behind.

We don't need to go overboard on transparency but some information should be readily available to patients. Let's start with physicians. I believe that at minimum, the following information about physicians should be easily accessible to patients:

1. Name of his/her medical school and the year of graduation
2. Information on internship and residency
3. Information on specialty board certification
4. Information about continuing medical education during the most recent five years
5. Results of patient satisfaction surveys

If the physician is a surgeon, the following additional information should either be posted or easily accessible by telephone:

1. Total number of each surgical procedure performed in the most recent year
2. The return-to-surgery rate for each procedure (The return-to-surgery rate is the percent of cases that are operated, dismissed from the surgery unit, and returned to surgery because of complications)
3. The surgeon's post-operative infection rate (The percent of patients who acquire an infection following the surgery)
4. The average length (time) of each surgical procedure

5. Severity adjusted* morbidity (complications) and mortality (death) rates
6. The surgeon's preferred anesthesiologist(s)

*Severity adjustment takes into account various conditions that may increase the morbidity and/or mortality rates associated with a procedure. For example, a complex surgery on an 85-year-old with diabetes and a history of heart disease has a much higher risk of complications and/or death than the same surgery on an otherwise healthy 30-year-old. Severity adjustment is critical for any kind of "report card" on healthcare providers. It applies to physicians as well as hospitals. Without severity adjustment, report cards can cause physicians and hospitals to avoid caring for the most complicated and highest risk patients and that would be a disservice to everyone.

Now let's take a look at hospitals. The following information should be available about hospitals:

1. The most recent Joint Commission on Accreditation of Healthcare Organizations (JCAHO) and/or Medicare survey results
2. Hospital-acquired infection rates
3. Readmission rates
4. Return-to-surgery rates
5. Severity-adjusted morbidity and mortality rates
6. Case Mix Index (a system that evaluates the complexity of the cases cared for at the hospital)
7. Number of patients transferred to another hospital
8. Number of patients transferred to the hospital from other hospitals
9. Number of patient care hours (Registered Nurse hours per patient day) by type of service, i.e., obstetrics, pediatrics, medical intensive care, surgical intensive care, cardiac intensive care, general medical unit, etc.
10. Average years of experience of nursing staff by type of service

11. Number of medical staff physicians that have had disciplinary actions taken against them in the most recent five years
12. Results of patient satisfaction surveys

For ambulatory surgery centers, the same information should be available as for hospitals, although the accrediting agency will be different and the question regarding transfers to other hospitals would change to reflect the number of patients transferred to a hospital. Additionally, the hospital(s) with which the surgery center has transfer agreements should be listed.

For freestanding diagnostic and treatment centers (imaging centers, laboratories, cancer treatment centers, etc.) the accrediting body survey results should be available as well as patient satisfaction survey results.

As healthcare becomes more consumer-driven, I expect that additional quality information will become available as physicians and hospitals compete for patients. For example, if hospitals are competing for heart surgeries, the hospital in the area with the highest quality indicators for that service will want to use that data in selling the value of their services to the customer. Competition based on price, quality and service is the only way to bring prices down while preserving consumer choice.

HEALTH INSURANCE PLANS PUBLISH HOW MUCH THEY WILL PAY

When you look at an explanation of benefits (EOB) from your insurance plan you will see what the charges were and how much the insurance plan paid. For each service provider the insurance plan establishes a price it will pay for each product or service. The amount they will pay varies from city to city and from provider to provider. Some variation is certainly understandable. Costs of land, labor, transportation, etc. are more in big cities than in small cities or towns. Teaching hospitals offer more services and have higher overhead than small hospitals. Despite these variations we need our insurance plans to be at least as transparent as we are asking the doctors, hospitals and pharmacies to be.

With the advent of Health Maintenance Organizations (HMOs) and Preferred Provider Organizations (PPOs) you may not have encountered the term "Reasonable and Customary Charge" in recent years. About the only time you may hear about it is if you go out of network in an HMO or PPO type plan. Insurance companies can use different approaches to arrive at their reasonable and customary table but in essence they collect charge information from the providers in a geographic area. This gives them a range of prices for each service and then they will pay up to some percentage of that range. The percent paid varies but it is fairly common for it to be around 80 percent. This price can be based on the International Classification of Disease (ICD-10-CM) Codes or Diagnosis Related Groups (DRGs). Payments are based on the final diagnosis and not the diagnosis at time of admission. About 75 percent of the time the admitting diagnosis is also the final diagnosis so if people shop for services based on DRGs there is a 25 percent chance that the final price will be different than they may have expected. Regardless, getting prices out there gives people the opportunity to make informed decisions regarding the differences between various hospitals. We're not talking about emergencies here. Based on data from the U.S. Department of Health and Human Services, the Center for Disease Control, the National Center for Health Statistics and the American Hospital Association about nine percent of emergency department visits result in hospital admission. These admissions through the emergency department represent approximately 35 percent of hospital admissions leaving about 65 percent that are scheduled admissions. The scheduled admissions are the ones the individual has the opportunity to influence.

If we want to get serious about driving prices down the insurance companies need to do develop what I'll call a Reasonable and Customary Price and base it on tables constructed from the contract prices they have from providers in the area. Once the price is established there is really no need for networks that keep people captive to certain doctors, hospitals and pharmacies, etc. The maximum price is established and that is all the insurance plan will pay.

GIVE CONSUMERS AN INCENTIVE TO GET INVOLVED

Once consumers know how much their insurance plan will pay, the stage is set for real competition to start working. Just because an insurance plan has established its Reasonable and Customary Price that doesn't mean a provider has to charge that much. If they want to compete for business they can drop their price. The only effective way to incentivize individuals to shop for healthcare services is to hit the pocketbook. If the amount the insurance plan will pay for a product or service, then the consumer can shop for a price lower than that. The incentive will come in the form of sharing the difference between the insurance plan price and the price the consumer finds or negotiates. This will need to be a three-way share with one-third going to the insurance company and two-thirds going to the individual and in the case of an employer provided plan, the employer. For employer based plans the two-thirds share should be split between the employee and the employer based on the percentage of premiums paid by each. For example, if the employer pays 80 percent of the premium and the employee pays 20 percent then the employer would get 80 percent of the savings. Of course, if the employer wants to encourage employee involvement in negotiating prices, then they can reward the employee with more of the savings. To avoid tax issues, I suggest the savings be given to the employee in the form of applying the savings to the employee's share of the premium.

INCLUDE INCENTIVES FOR INDIVIDUALS TO CARE ABOUT HEALTH STATUS

First, I need to address an issue that may not fit in this section, but I have to talk about emergencies someplace. Let's put aside emergency situations when talking about consumer choice in healthcare. Emergencies are emergencies and individuals need to seek the nearest medical help available. There is no time to shop in emergencies. On the other hand, most medical expenses are not emergencies. The majority of physician visits, surgeries, and hospitalizations have some element of flexibility and shopping is possible.

When you are using an HSA plan, you are spending some of your own money and have an incentive to conserve your resources. Assuming the plan shares savings with you so you have an incentive to shop and negotiate prices. Now, for the balance of this section, assume that you are the chief executive officer of your business and look at incentives from the perspective of your employer.

You want your employees to take care of themselves. Obesity, high blood pressure, smoking, elevated cholesterol levels, etc. contribute to increased healthcare costs. For example, "Researchers say that 56.4% of American adults were overweight in 2000, compared to 45% in 1991. According to the Centers for Disease Control and Prevention (CDC), 65.5% of men and 47.6% of women were overweight in 2000. The percentage of adults with diabetes increased from 4.9% in 1990 to 7.3% in 2000 and to 9.4% in 2015. Adult diabetes is 90% preventable if people exercise more, eat healthier food and adopt other healthy behaviors.

A study of 85,000 female nurses found that women who exercised for seven or more hours per week were half as likely to develop diabetes as women who exercised for less than half an hour weekly."[63] At the time of a 2002 study[64], the average adult had about $1,500 in

---

[63] "Obesity and Diabetes," National Center for Policy Analysis, NCPA Policy Digest, September 21, 2001.

[64] "Health-Care Costs Per Person for Obesity Exceed Smoking," National Center for Policy Analysis, NCPA Policy Digest, March 12, 2002.

healthcare expenses each year. Obesity added $395 a year to those costs, smoking added $230, and problem drinking added $150. Just being overweight but not obese added $125 per year. With the increased cost of healthcare since that study was performed, those costs have gone up considerably.

On an annual basis, individuals who volunteer to participate in an incentive program could have their weight, blood pressure, glucose, carbon monoxide (smokers have elevated carbon monoxide levels)[65] and lipid profile results evaluated for financial incentives. For each parameter that falls within the acceptable range, a financial incentive could be credited to the individual's HSA or applied as a credit toward future premiums. Don't be stingy, however. Voluntary wellness programs will generally have 15-20% participation. Wellness programs with financial incentives can achieve 70-90% participation. I recommend giving each individual a minimum of $100 cash just for doing the screening and then provide much larger HSA/Premium incentives based on maintaining healthy lifestyles. Insurance companies should be able to provide some guidance for incentive programs. Also, there are colleges, universities, hospitals, clinics, and businesses with an established wellness and/or incentive program that can be used as models.

COMPETITION DRIVEN BY PRICE, QUALITY, AND SERVICE—NOT NETWORKS

There are only two things I can add to what I have written previously about networks —reinforcement and a goal.

First, the reinforcement I believe that networks are among the greatest hoaxes perpetrated on the American public. I use "network" to describe Preferred Provider Organizations (PPOs), Physician Hospital Organizations (PHOs) and the myriad of Other Weird Arrangements (OWAs) that fool you into thinking they are saving

---

[65] Middleton, Edward T., "Breath Carbon Monoxide as an Indication of Smoking Habit." American College of Chest Physicians, March, 2000.

you money (I'd like to credit the originator of the wonderful term OWA, but I have not been able to identify who used the term first). What networks actually do is force physicians, hospitals and other providers of healthcare services to increase their prices so they can discount them. This creates a highly inflated price that imposes a severe penalty on those individuals who self-pay for services. So, the bottom line is, networks increase prices for the poor and self-insured, increase administrative costs, makes you unhappy by telling you which physicians and hospitals you should use, and they charge you a per member per month fee to obtain a price that a consumer-driven system will produce for free.

Now the goal I propose is the nationwide elimination of all networks by December 31, 2029. Phase them out. They are not needed. Once price, quality and service information is available, and the healthcare consumer has the proper incentives to care about price, utilization and health status, everything else will take care of itself.

REAL-TIME ELECTRONIC ADJUDICATION OF CLAIMS LINKING AN IDENTIFICATION DEBIT CARD/CREDIT CARD TO THE HSA AND THE INSURANCE PLAN

We mentioned this earlier but it warrants being repeated here as we bring things together to fix healthcare. An individual's insurance identification card can be a Medical Credit/Debit Card (MCDC) linked to the individual's HSA and the insurer. The MCDC can be scanned at the physician's office, imaging center, laboratory, surgical center, pharmacy, hospital, etc. The amount authorized (Reasonable and Customary Price) for the service being performed is displayed immediately and the healthcare service provider can explain to the patient the charges and how they compare with the approved amount.

The healthcare service provider is paid immediately through the MCDC with the charges going electronically to the patients HSA, and the insurer. The insurer credits the HSA with the appropriate payment, including any shared savings, and the HSA reduces the MCDC balance up to the amount in the HSA. If a balance remains, the patient would have the same options as they do with any other credit card. That is, pay it off when a statement is received or make monthly payments with interest accruing on the unpaid balance. This system will not work quite the same for inpatient hospital stays since the DRG is determined after the patient is discharged. However, the MCDC can be scanned at the time of admission, and as soon as the DRG is entered, all transactions will be completed immediately.

The MCDC could be issued by the government, the insurance plan, or a commercial bank. However, the interest rate charged on the MCDC must be kept at a low rate and should be linked to something like the 10-year Treasury Note or the Prime Rate. Maybe the Prime Rate plus one or two percent would be a good place to start.

PRE-CERTIFICATION AND CASE MANAGEMENT BY EXCEPTION

A few years ago I was meeting with a group of 30 – 35 physicians and I asked them how long it had been since they had been denied when requesting pre-certification for a procedure or a hospitalization. Most were mumbling to each other statements like, "I can't remember my last denial, have you had any recently?" After a short time an orthopedic surgeon with 35 or so years of experience said, "I've never been denied, but I have a full-time nurse who does nothing but make phone calls asking,

'Mother, May I?"

Several weeks later I was in the company of a health insurance company executive and I asked him, "How often do you deny requests for pre-certification?" He responded, "It is very rare!"

I followed with what he had to think was a stupid question when I asked, "If it is rare for you to deny a pre-certification, why do you require it?" He told me that although it is rare for them to deny a request, there are a lot of people who don't ask, and if someone does not ask, we can penalize them $500–$1,000 for not complying with that requirement. In other words, the primary use of the process was to save the insurance company money by penalizing people for not asking, "Mother, May I?"

My experience is that most physicians are sincere in their efforts to practice cost-effective medicine. They are sensitive to the costs borne by their patients and they discuss costs, benefits, and options with them. With all of the information available to (Third Party Administrators) TPAs and insurers, it is not difficult to identify the physicians, hospitals and other providers whose practice patterns are outside the norm. It is those providers that need to be monitored and required to jump through the hoops and over the hurdles of pre-certification and concurrent review when treating patients.

Identifying these providers and noting that they are subject to pre-certification and concurrent review provides additional impetus for them to "get their act together." These providers can be identified at the point of service when the patient's MCDC is processed.

We need to reward the practitioners that practice good, cost-effective medicine by removing the encumbrances and reaping the administrative cost savings in the process.

INSURANCE POOLS FOR THOSE WITH PRE-EXISTING CONDITIONS

The concept of insurance is for large numbers of people to each take a little risk to protect all against catastrophic loss. People buy fire insurance for their home and hope they never have to collect on it. They buy it for protection against the loss from a fire or other catastrophe. People buy life insurance, not to protect themselves from death, but to protect their families from the financial catastrophe of their premature death. Automobile insurance is purchased to protect the owner from the catastrophic loss associated with a collision, theft, fire, etc. Automobile insurance does not pay for routine oil changes, brakes, engine repairs, tires, etc. It is for catastrophic losses. Protection against catastrophic loss is a concept that has been lost in healthcare insurance. Healthcare insurance is now expected to

112

pay for everything! This move has taken place pretty much with the blessings of everyone—employees who always want the employer (in this case, the employer-sponsored healthcare insurance plan) to pay more; the employer that increases healthcare benefits to keep pace with the plans of other employers competing for the same labor force; the government(s) that mandate that more services be covered by insurance plans; and insurance companies that have added benefits to make plans more attractive.

Since we've gotten to where we are somewhat by consensus, let's recognize that healthcare insurance is no longer a pure insurance product (risk sharing for protection against a catastrophic loss) but that it has become a vehicle for financing most healthcare services in the United States. If we hope to gain any control over the increasing costs of healthcare, it is time to change some things.

Under our current structure that relies heavily on employer-sponsored healthcare insurance, healthcare is an employer issue first, an employee (individual) issue second, a community issue third, a regional issue fourth, a state issue fifth, and a national (federal government) issue sixth. This is wrong. The focus of healthcare should be on the individual and on improving the health status of the community. It is fine for employers to help finance the system and for state and federal governments to set policy and help the marginalized. But let's adjust the system so that the dog is wagging the tail.

One of the first things we need to do is stop shifting costs all over the place. When medical services are provided, costs are incurred and someone will pay those costs. In most cases, the businesses and residents of the community in which the services are provided will pay the costs.

We can minimize the need for huge insurance rate increases for pre-existing conditions by having a few large pools for sharing the risk of those with pre-existing conditions. I am a firm believer in community' and states' rights, so I believe the primary pools should be at the community and state levels.

I envision three pools working together. The first pool is at the community or area level and is the one that most closely reflects the health status, practice patterns, and service utilization by the individuals who live and work in the area. This is the pool from which claims of up to $250,000 are paid. The second pool is at the state level and all community pools would pay into the state pool. The state pool would serve two purposes. The first function would be to insure claims between $250,000 and $1,000,000, and the second would be to bridge the coverage of individuals moving between community pools. The third pool would be a national pool that would insure claims in excess of $1,000,000.

The actual number of pools is not really all that important and the actuaries can argue about the number of pools and whether the suggested insurance levels of the pools should be modified. What is important is that the pools be large enough and that they be composed of all individuals and businesses in a defined risk-sharing geographic area. These pools should also include government employees.

A community rating system is one that spreads the risk of insuring people that are seriously ill across all individuals in the pool. I am suggesting that we use that system for those with pre-existing conditions. The individuals with pre-existing conditions would have a premium based on community rating and a small amount of the premiums paid by all insureds would go to the aforementioned pools. The cost of healthcare insurance should not cause an employer to choose a less qualified employee because health insurance would cost too much for the better-qualified 55+ year old candidate or the one that has a chronic illness like diabetes.

Not returning to a community rating system (to establish premiums for those with pre-existing conditions) will lead to increased disparity between two groups of people—those who are well and those who are sick. The sick will be covered by some high risk pool with premiums so high that people can't afford to be in it. The other option is that it will be heavily subsidized by tax revenues and administered by bureaucrats. If that is the direction people want to go then give those with pre-existing conditions an option to buy into Medicare. Whatever the case, we need a rational system for keeping premiums as low as possible for healthy people while spreading the cost for the sick over the entire population.

I have heard people argue that young people that do not use many healthcare resources should pay lower premiums. I don't totally buy the argument. Healthcare insurance should be about keeping people healthy and protecting all against catastrophic loss. Older people may have more catastrophic loss due to heart disease and orthopedic problems, but young people have catastrophic losses due to injuries and having babies that require neonatal intensive care services. We are all in this together regardless of our age.

The objective is to create pools that have high percentages of the people remaining in the same pool for many years—for some, it will be decades or entire working careers. These pools also need to reflect the general economics of the region they cover. There are geographic variations in healthcare delivery and costs for delivery vary widely from rural to metropolitan areas. People who chose to live and conduct business in a rural Indiana town should not have to excessively subsidize, through their insurance premiums, the higher costs of providing care for those who choose to live and conduct business in New York City or Los Angeles for example.

Keeping people in the same pool regardless of which business they work for, or which insurance company administers their healthcare plan, has several cost saving advantages. First, if people stay in the same pool, the need for, and expense of, underwriting goes away. So does the need to penalize pre-existing conditions. The bottom line is, the businesses and individuals in the pool are going to share the risk for the necessary medical expenses incurred by members of the pool, and that sharing is going to be done in the most cost effective manner possible. That means, fewer cost shifting games.

Another advantage for keeping people in the same pool for many years is that there is an incentive for all pool participants to focus on activities with the potential to generate long-term savings for the pool. Today, most insurance companies, and employers, give lip service at best to programs that focus on preventive healthcare and healthy life styles. This is understandable, because those programs can take

20 years or more to pay-off in savings. With people moving in and out of insurance pools like they are today, there is little reason for an insurance company to spend money to help you avoid medical expenses 20 years down the road when, in all probability, they won't be insuring you when the pay-off comes.

SECURE HEALTH INFORMATION SYSTEM CONTROLLED BY THE INDIVIDUAL

We live in a highly mobile society and individuals move from job to job frequently. For those who stay with a company for several years, it is increasingly common for them to be moved from one business location to another. Whenever an individual moves from one community to another they have no choice but to change physicians, hospitals, and other healthcare providers. Added to that is the number of times people have to change physicians and/or hospitals because of changes in employer healthcare insurance plans and networks.

The result of this mobility, and the changes in healthcare providers, is that most people have multiple medical records that may be scattered around the country and the world. Although a medical record is the property of the provider, the medical information in that record belongs to the individual.

Creating a consolidated medical data file means that a healthcare provider can access pertinent medical information about an individual 24/7. In an emergency, the provider can view medical history, medications, family history, surgery, laboratory, and radiology reports and other information that can lead to a more rapid, more accurate diagnosis and a more efficacious treatment. In some cases, the availability of the information can avoid the unnecessary duplication of expensive diagnostic procedures.

Systems need to be available to the individual that allow the consolidation of medical information. That information needs to be encrypted for protection, the individual needs to be able to segment it so s/he can release only the necessary information, and the information needs to be available to authorized providers 24/7. Participating in such a system will enable patients to move more easily among the providers of choice, improve the quality of medical care, and avoid many of the costs associated with the duplication of diagnostic procedures.

CONCLUSION

In 1998 our Healthcare Expense Reduction Organization (HERO Healthcare, LLC) undertook the development of a consumer-driven health insurance pilot program in our community. We had discount contracts with a hospital and about 85 percent of the physicians in the area. The hospital was paid based on Diagnosis Related Groups and physician and other services were based on CPT code pricing. After meeting with 35 or 36 insurance companies we found one in Kansas City that agreed to work with us and abide by our "rules" that included, among other things, limiting their profits and agreeing to pay our fee schedule prices to any provider even if we did not have a contract with the provider. Another rule was that if a person insured under the plan could negotiate a price lower than our established price or find a provider outside the area that charged less than our price, then the difference in price would be shared by the insurance company, and the patient and the patient's employer in the form of premium credits. There were some formulas used to protect the insurance company and provisions for emergencies both locally and in other areas but the program gave individuals the incentive to care about cost.

We published all of our prices so individuals could easily determine what the insurance plan would pay. One day I received a call from a young lady (about 25 years old as I recall) telling me that she had been seen by an ears, nose and throat (ENT) specialist and that he had recommended she have her tonsils and adenoids removed but he would not accept our price schedule (by the way, he owned his own surgery center). She asked what she should do. I told her she could go to him and pay the $70 difference or she could go to an ENT with whom we had a contract. She told me she liked her doctor but not $70 worth and chose to go to one of the several ENTs that had agreed to accept our prices. It's interesting to note that the day after the young lady called her "old" doctor to have her medical records transferred to the "new" doctor, the "old" doctor called and joined our plan and began accepting our published prices.

It was a couple of weeks later that she called to tell me that she had been seen by doctor X and that he was very nice and spent almost an hour with her explaining why she didn't need her tonsils and adenoids removed. She said, "For the first time in my life I feel like I am in control of my healthcare! Thank you!" That was one of the most rewarding experiences I have had and is why I sincerely believe that regardless of how hard and frustrating it will be to build such a system nationwide it will be worth it.

We have a choice. We can continue going down the healthcare path we have traveled for decades, we, the people, can create change, or we can sit idly by and let politicians and special interests dictate the changes that benefit them first and us second. The historical path has led to a non-system with extremely high costs that leave many people uninsured at any given time.

There are essentially two choices for change. The first is to create a consumer-driven healthcare system. A properly designed system can reduce administrative costs, create competition based on price, quality, and service; provide a foundation for restructuring Medicare, and include those covered by Medicaid and the uninsured.

The second choice is a single-payer national health plan run by the government that will result in extended waiting times for specialized services and potentially rationing based on age, diagnosis or other criteria. Some are now advocating Medicare for all including illegal residents the economic impact of which is incomprehensible and would guarantee rationing in one form or another. Examine the Veteran's Administration system and then make your choice.

I suggest we begin by the government providing $200 million to a group of three or four states to develop and pilot the consumer-driven system as described above. The states of Indiana, Ohio, Kentucky and Michigan would be good candidates for the project. They are adjacent to each other which should make the logistics of working together simple and they offer diverse business communities and populations. They are also home to some of our top rated universities that could be very helpful with the project. Some banks already offer health savings accounts linked to a credit card or debit card and even allow some of the savings to be invested in mutual funds. Seems to me that a lot of the pieces are already in place and we just need to bring them together. According to Americans for Tax Reform it cost $4.5 billion to build the Affordable Care Act (Obamacare) state exchange websites alone. The success of the program is still being debated. Spending $200 million (or a little more if necessary) to try a consumer driven system before sinking-in over our heads with single-payer healthcare seems like a risk worth taking.

A national healthcare plan will be run by the government and will result in extended waiting times for specialized services and potentially rationing based on age, diagnosis or other criteria. Some are now advocating Medicare for all including illegal residents the economic impact of which is incomprehensible and would guarantee rationing in one form or another. Examine the Veteran's Administration system and then make your choice.

The choice is yours and you will make a choice. You will choose to create change by taking action, or you will choose to let change happen by ignoring the problem. Choose what you want for your children, your grandchildren, and beyond—a system in which the tail wags the dog, or a system in which the dog wags the tail. Chapter Seven covers what needs to be done. All we need is the political will to make it happen. Get involved or accept without complaint what others dictate!

OTHER REFERENCES

- Differences between ICD-10-CM, CPT, ICD-10-PCS, HCPCS coding; Velan Healthcare, January 23, 2018
- Burris, Alexandria, Health insurance exchange aims to bring up to 500 jobs to Indy, Indianapolis Star USA TODAY NETWORK
- Butcher, Lola, Six Things Consumers Will Know About You, AHA Speakers Bureau, June 9, 2015
- O'Donnell, Jayne, Deadly errors, infections: When hospital ratings don't align what should patients believe?, USA TODAY, May25, 2019
- Safety in Numbers, The Leapfrog Group's Report on High-Risk Surgeries Performed at American Hospitals
- The 10 Questions You Should Know, Agency for Healthcare Research and Quality, September, 2012
- Patient Satisfaction, Healthgrades.com
- Medicaid.gov

- Gingrich, Newt, On Drug Prices, Trump Should Heed Reagan's Advice: "Bold Colors" not "Pale Pastels," July 17, 2019
- Alonso-Zaldivar, Ricardo, Meals for seniors could save Medicare money, Associated Press
- Alonso-Zaldivar, Ricardo, Despite political rhetoric, system not melting down, Associated Press, July 26, 2019
- Riechert, Julia; Weil, Michael, Get Paid for Getting Dressed? Supreme Court Clarifies "Changing Clothes" Under the FLSA, Orrick Employment Law and Litigation
- CMS.gov
- Hunt, Janet, What Is the Origin of Insurance?, bizfluent, September, 26, 2017
- Stossel, John, Government Controlled Health Care Means Waiting Lines, Serious Drawbacks, ABC News, June 26, 2009
- Jost, Timothy, Affordability: The Most Urgent Health Reform Issue For Ordinary Americans, Health Policy Lab, February 29, 2016
- Sederer, Lloyd, Take Action Against Addiction, U.S. News and World Report, February 1, 2016
- Drugs, Brains, and Behavior, The Science of Addiction, National Institute on Drug Abuse, July 2018
- Desjardins, Jeff, How Americans Make and Spend Money, Money, March 19, 2019
- What Is the Government's Role in US Health Care?, Harvard Business School, Working Knowledge, March 2, 2007
- Chakraborty, Barnini, Health policy analyst: Democrats' so-called 'moderate' plan would 'effectively end' private healthcare, Fox News.com, May 15, 2019
- Malcolm, Candice, The Pitfalls of Single-Payer Health Care: Canada's Cautionary Tale, April 13, 2017
- Democrats and Republicans Agree: Take Politics out of Health Policymaking, Health, June 18, 2019

- Oliver, Wayne, Ending Defensive Medicine Is Key To Containing Health Care Costs, Investor's Business Daily, March 24, 2017
- Epstein, Lita, 6 Reasons Healthcare Is So Expensive in the U.S., Investopedia, February 4, 2019
- Measuring Health Care Quality: An Overview of Quality Measures, Families USA, May 2014
- Burkes, Norris, Sometimes, uncertainty is the only certainty, USA TODAY, June 1, 2019
- Rudavsky, Shari, Health care costs in state exceed neighboring states, Indianapolis Star USA TODAY NETWORK, April 29, 2019
- Court, Emma, Here's why Darapriim still costs $750 a pill, MarketWatch, February 4, 2016
- Insulin Costs Are Skyrocketing. This is why, health.usnews.com, June 29, 2018
- Hayward, Jeff, 6 Ways to Foster Healthy Social Skills in Children, Active Beat, January 21, 2016
- Mental Health Facts, Stats, and Data, mentalhealthamerica.net/issues/state-mental-health-america, Septermber 17, 2015
- Raphelson, Samantha, How The Loss Of U.S. Psychiatric Hospitals Led To A Mental Health Crisis, National Public Radio, November 30, 2017
- Number of hip replacements UK, charm, January 13, 2014
- Statistics of joint replacement surgery, maxx AESCULRP, January 21, 2013
- Davis, Karen; Stremikis, Kristof; Squires, David; Schoen, Cathy, Mirror, Mirror on the Wall, 2014 Update: How the U.S. Health Care System Compares Internationally, commonwealthfund.org, June 16, 2014
- Health care in Canada, Government of Canada, May 3, 2019
- Healthcare in England, Wikipedia.org/wiki/Healthcare_in_England; May 1, 2019
- Pros and Cons of Universal Health Care in Canada, Form+sa Post, December 2016

- Pipes, Sally, Say No To Canadian Drug Imports, Associated Press, April 29, 2019
- Light, Donald W., Global Drug Discovery: Europe Is Ahead, Health Affairs volume 28, No. 5: BENDING THE COST CURVE, September/October 2009
- Pros and Cons of Private Health Care, Form+sa Post, November 25, 2016
- Alltucker, Ken, 1.1M more in US lost health coverage, USA TODAY, May 10, 2019
- Total health expenditure per capita in Canada from 1975 to 2018 (in Canadian dollars), The Statistics Portal
- Country comparison United States vs United Kingdom, countryeconomy.com/countries/compare
- Management of MRI Wait Lists in Canada, Health Policy, February 2009
- Total number of magnetic resonance imaging (MRI) units in the United Kingdom (UK) from 2000-2014, The Statistics Portal
- Number of magnetic resonance imaging (MRI) units in selected countries as of 2017, The Statistics Portal
- McFarlane, Greg, The Drawbacks Of Single-Payer Healthcare, Facebook, Twitter, Linkedin, November 28, 2013
- Access to Health Services, HealthyPeople.gov; 2017
- Pipes, Sally, Britain's Version Of Medicare For All' Is Struggling With Long Waits For Care, April 1, 2019
- Bukata, Richard, MD: CT Overuse: The Problem Beneath the Problem, Emergency Physicians Monthly, December 31, 2015
- Over 75 Million CT Scans Are Performed Each Year and Growing Despite Radiation Concerns, iData Research, August 29, 2018
- Kashef, Ziba, Yale University, Overuse of Medical Services Increases Healthcare Costs, SciTechDaily, June 29, 2015
- Letourneau, Rene, Defensive medicine adds billions to healthcare costs, November 4, 2011

- Graedson, Terry, How Much does It Really Cost to Develop a New Drug?, The Peoples Pharmacy, September 14, 2017
- Finnegan, Joanne; Study highlights long wait times in Canada under single-payer system, Does that make it bad idea for U.S.?, FierceHealthcare!, December 11, 2018
- Pipes, Sally, Heed the cautionary tale of Canadian health care, Pacific Research Institute, January 24, 2019
- Five ways to reduce healthcare administrative costs, managedhealthexecutive.com, August 24, 2017
- Cutler, David, PhD, Wikler, Elizabeth, B.A.; Basch, Peter, MD; Reducing Administrative Costs and Improving the Health Care System, New England Journal of Medicine, November 15, 2012
- Cutler, David M., 3 Strategies for Reducing Health Care Administrative Costs, Center for American Progress, June 11, 2012
- "Managed Care Options Running Out." National Center for Policy Analysis, Daily Policy Digest, Thursday, May 10, 2001.
- Crossette, Barbara, "Canada's Health Care Shows Strains." The New York Times, October 11, 2001.
- Kuttner, Robert, "The American Health Care System – Wall Street and Health Care." The New England Journal of Medicine, February 25, 1999, Volume 340, Number 8.
- Pear, Robert, "Doctors Shunning Patients With Medicare." The New York Times, March 17, 2002.
- "Budget Time Comes to Welfare States." National Center for Policy Analysis, 2001. http://www.ncpa.org/health/pdh49.html.
- Lyall, Sarah, "94-Year-Old Becomes Case Study in British Health Care Woes." The New York Times, January 26, 2002.
- "Scots Will Wait No More Than Nine Months for Treatment." National Center for Policy Analysis, NCPA Policy Digest, January 5, 2001.
- "Canadian Health System in Decline." National Center for Policy Analysis, NCPA Policy Digest, February 5, 2001.

- Kuttner, Robert, "The American Health Care System – Employer-Sponsored Health Coverage." The New England Journal of Medicine, January 21, 1999, Volume 340, Number 3.
- Herrick, Devon, "The Gore Health Proposal: One Step Forward, Three Steps Back." National Center for Policy Analysis, Brief Analysis #308, December 3, 1999.
- Iglehart, John K. "The American Health Care System – Medicaid." The New England Journal of Medicine, February 4, 1999, Volume 340, Number 5.
- "Veterans' Pharmacy Benefit Program Restricts Access to New Drug Therapies." National Center for Policy Analysis, NCPA Policy Digest, October 4, 2000.
- "Hospital Competition Lowers Cost." National Center for Policy Analysis, NCPA Policy Digest, March 22, 2000.
- "About FACCT." http://www.facct.org/about.html.
- "Economist Says Drug Spending Not a Crisis." National Center for Policy Analysis, NCPA Policy Digest, April 6, 2001.
- "1988-1999 industry-wide results Gropu Accident & Health lines from all Life-Health underwriters." A.M. Best's Life and Health 1999 Aggregates and Averages.
- "Refundable Tax Credits Would Help the Uninsured." National Center for Policy Analysis, NCPA Policy Digest, December 4, 2001.
- "The government cut the price of vaccines. Now it's hard to find them." wysiwyg://4http://www.forbes.com/forbes/2002/0318/050_print.html.
- Scandlen, Greg. "Out of Control." February 26, 2002, http://www/showmenews.com/2002/Feb/20020226Comm066.asp.
- "Drug Companies Want to Give Away Free Samples." National Center for Policy Analysis, NCPA Policy Digest, November 15, 2000.
- "Consumer Information and Retail Prices for Prescription Drugs." National Center for Policy Analysis, NCPA Policy Digest, October 5, 2000.

- "Pharmacy Benefit Management." Healthcare Business Digest Online, http://www.mmhc.com/hebd/articles/HCBD9803/Pharmacy.html.
- "Biopharmaceuticals Offset their Expense by Reducing Health Care Costs." National Center for Policy Analysis, NCPA Policy Digest, March 26, 2002.
- "Newer Drugs Cut Overall Health Care Costs." National Center for Policy Analysis, NCPA Policy Digest, September 13, 2001.
- "Higher Health Care Costs: Who Cares?" National Center for Policy Analysis, NCPA Policy Digest, April 19, 2001.
- "Who Pays for Health Care?" National Center for Policy Analysis, NCPA Policy Digest, February 1, 2001.
- "Towers Perrin Survey finds Employers Committed to Playing an Active Role in Health Care Despite Concerns About rising Costs." http://www.towers.com/towers/news/dailynews/new1.html.
- HERO Healthcare, L.L.C, an Indiana Limited Liability Company, 1527 Kossuth Street, Lafayette, Indiana.
- "Behold the Power of Small Business." National Center for Policy Analysis, NCPA Policy Digest, February 21, 2002.
- "Solving the 'Free Rider' Problem in Health Insurance." National Center for Policy Analysis, NCPA Policy Digest, April 20, 2001.
- Appleby, Julie. "Hospitals fight for turf in medical arms race, Medical centers become more specialized to increase profits." USA TODAY, February 20, 2002.
- Rubin, Rita. "Soaring malpractice premiums stun many doctors." USA TODAY, December 4, 2001.
- "Medical Errors Common, Survey Reveals." National Center for Policy Analysis, NCPA Policy Digest, May 9, 2001.
- Appleby, Julie. "Pricey infertility care sparks insurance clash, Opponents resent higher premiums for coverage." USA TODAY, December 19, 2001.

- Bodenheimer, Thomas. "The American Health Care System – The Movement for Improved Quality in Health Care. The New England Journal of Medicine, February 11, 1999, Volume 340, Number 6.
- Freudenheim, Milt. "A New Health Plan May Raise Expenses for Sickest Workers." The New York Times, December 5, 2001.
- Gentry, Carol. "How Is Merrill Lynch Limiting Health Costs? By Expanding Benefits." The Wall Street Journal, May 23, 2000.
- Katt, Peter C. "Getting 'Real' with Health Care." Journal of Financial Planning, May, 2000.
- Krugman, Paul. "Bad Medicine." The New York Times, March 19, 2002.
- McClellan, Mark and Staiger, Douglas. "The Quality of Health Care Providers." NBER Working Paper No. W7327 Issued in August, 1999.
- Pauly, Mark V. and Hoff, John S. "Responsible Tax Credits for Health Insurance." The AEI Press, Washington, D.C., 2002.
- Raphael, Rebecca. "Giving Your Doctor a Checkup." http://abcnews.go.com/onair/2020/PRIMETIME_hmodoctors_001116_feature.html.
- Romell, Rick and Manning Joe. "Dose of political leadership is needed." Milwaukee Journal Sentinel, February 10, 2002.
- Swartz, Katherine, "Healthy New York: Making Insurance More Affordable for Low-Income Workers." The Commonwealth Fund. www.cmwf.org.
- Wachter, Robert M. and Goldman, Lee. "The Hospitalist Movement 5 Years Later." Journal of the American Medical Association, Volume 287, Number 4, January 23/30, 2002.
- "1999 Health Care Criteria for Performance Excellence." Baldrige National Quality Program.
- "Cost and Availability of Health Insurance for People with Chronic Health Conditions." National Association of Health Underwriters, 2002.

- "The Lumenos Program." http://www.lumenos.com/the_lumenos_program/Overview.
- "Supporting Quality-Based Decisions." http://www.facct.org/information.html.
- "Usual, Customary & Reasonable Fees." http://www.drjay.com/ucr.html.
- "Health Care 'Report Cards' May Increase Costs and Reduce Quality." National Center for Policy Analysis, Weekly Health Policy Digest, March 8, 2002.
- "IRS Hints Public Employers May do D-C Right Now." National Center for Policy Analysis, Scandlen's Health Policy Comments, February 25, 2002.
- "Oodles of news From Canada." National Center for Policy Analysis, Scandlen's Health Policy Comments, February 11, 2002.
- "Patients Learn to Haggle with Doctors Over Their Bills." National Center for Policy Analysis, NCPA Policy Digest, February 11, 2002.
- "Consumer-Driven Health Plans Gain in Popularity." National Center for Policy Analysis, NCPA Policy Digest, January 8, 2002.
- "Uninsured Who Pay Cash are Charged More Than Those With Health Insurance." National Center for Policy Analysis, NCPA Policy Digest, April 2, 2001.
- "By 2050 There Could be Nearly A Million Centenarians in the U.S." National Center for Policy Analysis, NCPA Policy Digest, May 3, 2001.
- "Drug Rationing Reduces Cancer Survival Rates in Britain." National Center for Policy Analysis, NCPA Policy Digest, May 8, 2001.
- "Canadian Women Wait for Breast Cancer Treatment." National Center for Policy Analysis, NCPA Policy Digest, May 14, 2001.
- "Illiteracy is Dangerous to Your Health." National Center for Policy Analysis, NCPA Policy Digest, March 30, 2000.

- "Market-Based Health Care." National Center for Policy Analysis, NCPA Policy Digest, June 1, 2000.
- "Patients, Doctors Could Benefit From Greater Use of the Internet." National Center for Policy Analysis, NCPA Policy Digest, July 26, 2000.
- "Emergency Room Shutdowns." National Center for Policy Analysis, NCPA Policy Digest, December 19, 2000.

ABOUT THE AUTHOR

Mr. Sanderson began his health care career at St. Elizabeth Medical Center, Lafayette, Indiana, in 1965, became a registered medical technologist, MT (ASCP) in 1966, and received his Bachelor of Science degree from Purdue University, West Lafayette, Indiana in 1967. He served as a medic in the United States Air Force Reserve and became licensed in life and health insurance in the state of Indiana in 1995.

From 1965 – 1975 he worked in the clinical and pathology laboratories of St. Elizabeth Medical Center and served in several capacities including research technologist, supervisor of the Department of Nuclear Medicine, Education Coordinator for the School of Medical Technology, Chief Medical Technologist, and Laboratory Manager. At various times while working in the laboratories, he served as Adjunct Assistant Professor of Medical Technology at Western Michigan University; lectured in health sciences classes and classes in the Department of Bionucleonics at Purdue University; and was Technical Associate Faculty at the

Indiana University School of Medicine, Lafayette Center for Medical Education at Purdue University.

From 1975 – 1995, he served in hospital administration first as an Administrative Assistant and later as Vice President. During his tenure in hospital administration, his duties included contract management, directing public relations, community relations, planning, marketing, physician relations, development, and data processing (information services). During this time he also served on the corporate computer center (Alverno Administrative Services) planning committee, and the Indiana Hospital Association Council on Data, and Public Relations committee. During this period he gave numerous talks on hospital and healthcare costs to various groups in the area, to Congressional representatives, and appeared on television debates and call-in shows focusing on healthcare costs. During a 1983 presentation to then Indiana 7th District Congressman John T. Meyer he stated that congress should allow tax exempt medical savings accounts as a way to get people more involved in healthcare purchases and save money for healthcare costs during retirement.

After leaving the hospital business in 1995, he, Mr. Randy Vernon, and Mr. Tom Hall formed Community Health and Benefits Associates, LLC in 1995 and he and Mr. Vernon formed HERO Healthcare, LLC in 1997 (HERO is an acronym for Healthcare Expense Reduction Organization). These businesses were formed to research healthcare cost issues (CH&BA) and to develop consumer-driven health care insurance plans for small businesses (HERO). He continues to research healthcare issues and speaks to groups when requested.

This work flows from his experiences, research, and observations during his more than 40 years in the health care business.

INDEX

Symbols

1/3 art, 1/3 science, and 1/3 luck 100

\"beef\" with insurance companies 14

A

About the Author 133

a country of laws 30, 97

actinic keratosis 38

Addiction 29

administrative costs xiii, 8, 9, 11, 12, 19, 51, 83, 110, 120, 127

Affordable Care Act 2, 23, 25, 78, 92

American Addiction Centers 28

a privilege 94

a right 94

B

benefit of mankind 34

biased against single payer 55

C

Canada 3, 5, 8, 55, 58, 124, 125, 126, 127, 131

Candidates are donor-driven 31

catastrophic loss 76, 84, 98, 112, 113, 115

charges have little, if anything, to do with cost 20

civics lessons 87

Clawbacks 38

community health centers 27

concept of insurance 83

consolidated medical data 116

coping skills 30

CPT 23

CT 41, 42, 56, 59, 87, 126

Current Procedural Terminology (CPT™) 24

D

Daraprim 35
Diagnosis Related Groups 24
didn't enjoy practicing medicine
    anymore 12
discount of $13,750.77 or 61.9% 21
DRG and CPT™ Pricing Structure 23
Drug Use 28

E

England xiv, 8, 56, 125, 127, 128, 130
ENT 120

F

FACCT 128
Families matter 32
first health insurance policies xiii

H

healthcare in the United States 91
Healthcare is a political \"hot
    potato\" 78
Health Savings Accounts 75, 76, 98
high blood pressure 39
Honor and integrity matter 32
HSA 19, 20, 98, 99, 100, 108, 109, 110
HSAs 76, 98

I

I am in control of my healthcare 120
insulin 34, 35
*Integrating Medical Record and Billing
    Systems* 13
itemized bills 45
*It's All About Money! However, some
    do care about mankind* 34

L

lack of education 93

Lasik surgery 86
lawsuit 40, 43
lawsuits 40, 43, 45, 50, 83

M

Mandatory Medicaid Benefits 95
Medicaid xiv, xv, 2, 5, 9, 12, 17, 18,
    25, 26, 27, 52, 62, 63, 80, 86,
    91, 92, 93, 94, 95, 96, 97, 120,
    123, 128
Medicare xiv, xv, 5, 9, 12, 17, 18, 27,
    39, 43, 52, 62, 63, 71, 76, 79, 80,
    86, 91, 92, 98, 102, 104, 120,
    124, 126, 127
mental health 27, 28, 29, 30, 33, 46,
    47, 48, 49
Moral courage matters 32
Most people do not yearn to be free.
    Most people yearn to be taken
    care of 44
Mother, May I 15, 19, 76, 111, 112
MRI 13, 15, 42, 56, 59, 62, 83, 87, 126

N

national health plan xv, 120
national health spending 1
networks xi, xiii, xv, 60, 64, 66, 67, 72,
    74, 75, 77, 82, 106, 109, 110, 116
Networks xiii
no connection between charge and
    price 21

O

optional benefits 95
organized labor 89

P

Patient Compensation System 43, 52
people do respond to incentives 85
physician shortage 79

www.ingramcontent.com/pod-product-compliance
Lightning Source LLC
Chambersburg PA
CBHW030750180526
45163CB00003B/965